easy desserts

easy desserts

deliciously indulgent treats

RYLAND
PETERS
& SMALL

LONDON NEW YORK

Designer Iona Hoyle
Senior Editor Julia Charles
Picture Research Emily Westlake
Production Toby Marshall
Art Director Leslie Harrington
Publishing Director Alison Starling

Indexer Hilary Bird

First published in Great Britain in 2009
by Ryland Peters & Small
20–21 Jockey's Fields
London WC1R 4BW
www.rylandpeters.com

10 9 8 7 6 5 4 3 2 1

ISBN 978 1 84597 815 0

A CIP record for this book is available
from the British Library.

Printed in China

Notes

• All spoon measurements are level
unless otherwise specified.

• Eggs are medium unless otherwise
specified. Uncooked or partly cooked
eggs should not be served to the
very young, the very old, those with
compromised immune systems or to
pregnant women.

contents

introduction

There really is nothing like a little self indulgence and everyone enjoys a good dessert but it is so often overlooked as the prospect of making one can seem a little daunting. This book offers the perfect solution. Here you'll find 100 no-fuss recipes for every occasion. Whether you want a warm and comforting winter pudding, an impressive party dessert for entertaining or something light and refreshing when dining al fresco on a summer's day, you'll find the perfect recipe here. The truly irresistible recipes include the best of British classics such as bread and butter pudding and sticky toffee pudding plus legendary American desserts such as key lime pie and peach cobbler. Chocoholics will find plenty to excite their tastebuds from chocolate amaretto torta to Mississippi mud pie. Pastry fans will not be disappointed either, with everything from hearty apple pie to a melt-in-the-mouth rhubarb galette to tempt them. With such a wealth of great recipes at your fingertips there's no excuse not to treat yourself and your family today and every day!

pies & tarts

apple pie

1 recipe American Pie Crust
(page 44)

6 tart eating apples, peeled, cored and
sliced ½ cm thick

6 sweet eating apples, peeled, cored
and sliced ½ cm thick

150 g caster sugar plus
1 tablespoon

2½ tablespoons cornflour

1 teaspoon grated lemon zest

1 tablespoon freshly squeezed
lemon juice

1 teaspoon ground cinnamon

¼ teaspoon ground cloves

½ teaspoon freshly
grated nutmeg

½ teaspoon salt

1 egg white

vanilla ice cream or pouring cream,
to serve

*a glass or ceramic pie dish,
23 cm diameter*

serves 8

Known in American diner slang as 'Eve with a lid on', apple pie is a beloved favourite in the USA. Although most people think of it as American, it was actually first made in England and taken there by colonists. It is delicious served warm with vanilla ice cream or chilled pouring cream.

Roll out half the pie dough and arrange in the pie dish. Set aside until needed. Roll out the remaining dough until it is a 30-cm disc. Transfer to a piece of greaseproof paper. Place both in the fridge, leaving at least 1 hour before filling.

Preheat the oven to 190°C (375°F) Gas 5. Put a baking tray inside to heat. To make the filling, toss the apples in a large mixing bowl with 150 g of the sugar, the cornflour, lemon zest and juice, cinnamon, cloves, nutmeg and salt. Pour into the uncooked pie case and cover with the rolled pastry. Press the edges together to seal. Tuck the dough underneath itself and press on to the rim of the dish. Crimp the edges of the pastry in a zigzag pattern. Cut 4 small slits in the pastry with a knife to let the steam out. Use any trimmings to decorate the top of the pie as desired. Brush the top with the egg white and sprinkle over the remaining tablespoon of sugar.

Bake the pie on the hot baking tray for 60 minutes, or until golden brown. Serve warm.

pumpkin pie

1 recipe American Pie Crust (page 44)
one 475-g tin pumpkin purée or 500 ml homemade pumpkin purée*
100 g light soft brown sugar
3 large eggs
200 ml evaporated milk
120 ml golden syrup
a good pinch of salt
1 teaspoon cinnamon
½ teaspoon mixed spice
1 teaspoon vanilla extract
2 tablespoons rum (optional)

2 tart tins or pie dishes, 22 cm diameter

serves 8–12

*To make the purée, cut a pumpkin or butternut squash into large chunks and bake for about 1 hour at 160°C (325°F) Gas 3. Scrape the flesh from the skin and purée until smooth in a food processor.

Tinned pumpkin purée gives a light, velvety result but if it's not available homemade pumpkin or butternut squash purée makes an acceptable substitute.

Bring the pastry to room temperature. Preheat the oven to 190°C (375°F) Gas 5.

Roll out the pastry thinly on a lightly floured work surface, then use to line the 2 tart tins or pie dishes. Trim and crimp or decorate the edges as you wish. Prick the bases all over with a fork, chill or freeze for 15 minutes.

To blind bake the pastry cases, line with foil or baking parchment then fill with baking beans. Set on a baking tray and bake blind in the centre of the oven for about 10–12 minutes. Remove the foil or baking parchment and the baking beans and return the pastry case to the oven for a further 5–7 minutes to dry out completely. To prevent the pastry from becoming soggy, brush the blind-baked case with beaten egg – you can do this when it is hot or cold. Bake again for 5–10 minutes until set and shiny. This will also fill and seal any holes made when pricking before blind baking.

Lower the oven to 160°C (325°F) Gas 3. Put all the filling ingredients into a food processor and blend until smooth. Pour into the pastry cases, set them on a baking tray and bake in the preheated oven for about 1 hour or until just set. Remove from the oven and let stand for 10 minutes, then remove the tart tins and let cool for a few minutes. Serve warm or at room temperature, not chilled.

blueberry & lime sour cream pie

1 recipe Pâte Brisée (page 43)
300 ml sour cream
2 tablespoons freshly squeezed lime juice
2 tablespoons Drambuie or other whisky liqueur
100 g caster sugar
¼ teaspoon ground cinnamon
¼ teaspoon ground allspice
a pinch of salt
2 large eggs, beaten
450 g fresh blueberries
100 ml lime marmalade

*a deep tart tin,
22 cm diameter, 3 cm deep*

serves 6

The combination of juicy blueberries and lime is terrific, especially when laced with the herby notes of Drambuie.

Bring the pastry to room temperature. Preheat the oven to 200°C (400°F) Gas 6.

Roll out the pastry thinly on a lightly floured work surface, then use to line the tart tin. Prick the base, then chill or freeze for 15 minutes. Bake blind following the method on page 12.

Lower the oven to 180°C (350°F) Gas 4 and put a baking tray in the oven to heat. Put the sour cream, lime juice, Drambuie, sugar, spices, salt and eggs into a large bowl and mix well. Put a single layer of blueberries into the pastry case and pour over the sour cream mixture.

Bake the tart on the preheated tray for 45 minutes until the filling is set and the pastry cooked. Remove from the oven and let cool. When cool, remove from the tart tin.

Melt the marmalade in a small saucepan and, when runny, strain through a sieve. Mix the rest of the blueberries with the marmalade and pile on top of the cooled pie. Chill for at least 1 hour, but remove from the fridge 15 minutes before serving.

key lime pie

1 recipe Sweet Tart Pastry
(page 42)

lime filling
4 eggs, separated
one 400-g tin sweetened
condensed milk
2 tablespoons grated lime zest
150 ml freshly squeezed lime juice
(from 5–6 limes)
¼ teaspoon cream of tartar

cream topping
250 ml whipping cream
3 tablespoons vanilla sugar*
zest of 1 large lime, pared
into fine shreds

a tart tin, 23 cm diameter

serves 6–8

The name of this classic American dessert comes from the
Florida Keys where once, until a hurricane destroyed many
of the orchards, limes were grown in adundance.

Roll out the pastry and use to line the tart tin. Bake blind following
the method given on page 42.

To make the lime filling, put 1 whole egg and 3 egg yolks in a bowl
and beat until blended. Whisk in the condensed milk and lime zest.
Gradually whisk in the lime juice.

Put the egg whites and cream of tartar in a separate, grease-free
bowl and whisk until stiff but not dry. Beat 2 tablespoons of the egg
white mixture into the egg yolk mixture, then fold in the remainder
with a spatula. Scrape into the pastry case and bake in a preheated
oven at 180°C (350°F) Gas 4 for about 20 minutes or until risen and
just firm in the centre. Remove from the oven and let cool in its tin
on a wire rack. It will deflate as it cools.

When cool, make the topping. Put the cream and 2 tablespoons of
the sugar in a bowl, whip until softly stiff, then spread over the lime
filling. Toss the shreds of lime zest in the remaining sugar and use to
decorate the tart. Serve cold but not chilled.

*To make the vanilla sugar, bury 2 or 3 vanilla pods in a jar of caster
sugar and leave for 1 week, after which the sugar will have taken
on the aroma of vanilla. Or, for a quick version, grind 3 tablespoons
caster sugar with a small piece of vanilla pod in a coffee grinder.

banoffi pie

one 225-g tin condensed milk

275 g digestive or other wheaten biscuits

100 g unsalted butter

3 bananas

200 ml double cream

30 g good-quality dark chocolate (minimum 70% cocoa solids)

a loose-based metal flan tin, about 20 cm diameter

serves 4

Very rich and delicious, banoffi pie is only for those with a very sweet tooth. Note that you'll need to let the condensed milk cool overnight so remember to start the preparation the day beforehand. Boil up several tins of condensed milk at once, then keep them in the cupboard until needed.

Put the unopened tin of condensed milk in a large saucepan. Cover with water, bring to the boil, then reduce the heat and simmer for 3 hours. Check the water level from time to time and top up as necessary. Let cool overnight.

Put the digestive biscuits in a blender or food processor and whizz until crushed.

Melt the butter in a small saucepan. Add the biscuit crumbs and mix well. Spoon the buttered crumbs into the flan dish and spread evenly over the bottom and up the sides, pressing down with the back of a spoon to form a firm crust. Place in the fridge to set.

Open the cooled tin of condensed milk to reveal the sticky caramel. Spoon it into the pie crust and spread out evenly.

Slice the bananas and lay them on top of the caramel layer. Pour the cream into a large bowl and whip until soft peaks form, then spoon it over the banana layer. Grate the chocolate and sprinkle it over the cream to decorate. Keep chilled until ready to serve.

hazelnut, chocolate & cardamom cream pie

hazelnut pastry
100 g hazelnuts
60 g unsalted butter, softened
25 g icing sugar
125 g plain flour, unsifted
1 egg yolk

filling
10 green cardamoms
300 ml double cream
200 g good-quality dark chocolate (minimum 70% cocoa solids), broken into chunks
25 g unsalted butter
1 tablespoon cocoa powder, sifted, to decorate

a fluted flan tin, 23 cm diameter

serves 8

You'll need to chill this delicious tart for at least two hours before serving. It is delicious served with a small glass of Frangelico, the hazelnut liqueur from Italy.

Preheat the oven to 190°C (375°F) Gas 5.

Spread the hazelnuts out on a baking tray and toast in the oven for 15 minutes or until lightly browned. Let cool, then chop in a food processor or coffee grinder. Cream the butter with the sifted icing sugar, add 40 g of the hazelnuts then gradually work in the flour. Beat the egg yolk with 1 tablespoon water and add to the mixture, gradually pulling it into a ball.

Turn out onto a floured board or work surface and roll or press it out gently into a round slightly smaller than the flan tin. Carefully lower it into the tin (don't worry if it breaks) and press it round and up the side until you have formed a pastry case. Chill in the fridge for at least half an hour, then prick the base and bake in the oven for about 15–20 minutes until lightly browned. Let cool.

Meanwhile, crush the cardamoms with a pestle in a mortar or with the end of a rolling pin. Remove the green husks and finely grind the seeds. Add to the cream and gently warm in a saucepan until the surface is just beginning to tremble. Don't let it boil. Take off the heat and add the chocolate chunks, butter and the remaining ground hazelnuts. Let cool, but don't let it get cold. Pour into the pastry case and put in the fridge for at least 2 hours. Dust the surface with cocoa powder just before serving.

mississippi mud pie

biscuit base
225 g digestive or other wheaten biscuits
60 g unsalted butter
60 g plain chocolate, finely chopped

chocolate filling
180 g plain chocolate, chopped
180 g unsalted butter, cut into small pieces
4 large eggs, beaten
90 g light muscovado sugar
90 g dark muscovado sugar
180 ml double cream

a springform cake tin, 23 cm diameter, well buttered

serves 8

This famous pie comes from the South of the USA – it is supposed to look like the thick, dark, muddy waters of the Mississippi Delta. Serve the pie in slices with generous spoonfuls of whipped cream.

To make the base, put the biscuits into a food processor and process to a fine crumb. Alternatively, put the biscuits into a plastic bag and crush with a rolling pin. Transfer the crumbs to a mixing bowl.

Put the butter and chocolate into a heatproof bowl set over a saucepan of steaming but not boiling water and melt gently (do not let the base of the bowl touch the water). Remove from the heat, stir gently, then stir into the biscuit crumbs. When well mixed, transfer the mixture to the prepared tin and, using the back of a spoon, press onto the base and about halfway up the sides of the tin. Chill in the fridge while making the filling.

To make the filling, put the chocolate and butter into a heatproof bowl set over a saucepan of steaming but not boiling water and melt gently (do not let the base of the bowl touch the water). Remove from the heat, stir gently, then let cool.

Preheat the oven to 180°C (350°F) Gas 4. Put the eggs and sugar into a large mixing bowl and, using an electric whisk or mixer, whisk until thick and foamy. Whisk in the cream followed by the melted chocolate. Pour the mixture into the biscuit case and bake in the preheated oven for about 45 minutes until just firm. Let cool for a few minutes then transfer to a plate and chill. Remove from the fridge 30 minutes before serving.

apple strudel

50 g amaretti biscuits (about 9)

4 tart eating apples (about 800 g), peeled, cored and sliced

70 g caster sugar

1½ teaspoons ground cinnamon

200 g filo pastry, defrosted if frozen

50 g unsalted butter, melted, plus extra for greasing

2 tablespoons slivered almonds or raisins or dried blueberries

icing sugar, for dusting

pouring cream or Greek-style yoghurt, to serve

serves 6

Ready-made filo pastry works well here, and it doesn't matter what it looks like when it goes into the oven. When it's baked and dusted with icing sugar, the strudel will taste and look sensational.

Preheat the oven to 200°C (400°F) Gas 6. Grease the baking tray with a little soft butter.

Put the amaretti biscuits into a plastic bag and crush them with the end of a rolling pin to form a fine crumb. Put the apple slices in a large bowl. Mix the sugar and cinnamon in another bowl.

Unwrap the pastry and separate the sheets. Overlap the sheets to make a rectangle about 55 x 70 cm. Using a pastry brush, lightly brush about half the melted butter over the pastry. Sprinkle the amaretti crumbs on top, then add the apple slices leaving a clear border of about 5 cm all around the edges. Sprinkle with the sugar and cinnamon mixture, then add the almonds or dried fruit.

To roll up the strudel, first fold over the pastry borders along the two short sides, then fold over the pastry border along one long side. Roll up the strudel from this side, and don't worry if the pastry splits and the filling falls out, just push it all back together with your hands. Transfer the roll to the buttered baking tray. Brush all over with the rest of the melted butter. Bake in the preheated oven for about 35 minutes, until golden brown. Dust with icing sugar, cut into thick slices and eat warm or at room temperature with pouring cream or Greek-style yoghurt.

apple & blueberry tarts

one 375-g sheet ready-rolled puff
pastry, defrosted if frozen

2 tablespoons caster sugar

1 vanilla pod, cut in half lengthways

3 sweet eating apples (such as Red
Delicious or Braeburn), each cored and
cut into 10–12 thin wedges

1 punnet blueberries (about 150 g)

double cream, to serve

serves 4–6

These are a cheat's delight – so simple and quick to make
and deliciously fresh-tasting. Any leftover tarts can be served
cold and enjoyed with coffee the next day. Just dust them
with some icing sugar and eat them as you would a fruit-
filled Danish pastry.

Take the pastry out of the fridge and let it rest for 20 minutes.

Unroll the pastry and cut it into 4–6 squares or rectangles of equal
size, as desired. Place these on a baking tray.

Put the sugar and 2 tablespoons of water in a saucepan and bring
to the boil, stirring until the sugar dissolves. Scrape the seeds from
the vanilla pod directly into the sugar syrup, stirring to combine.

Preheat the oven to 220°C (425°F) Gas 7.

Add the apple slices to the pan, reduce the heat to medium and
cook for 4–5 minutes, turning the apples so they cook evenly. Add
the blueberries and gently stir to coat them in the sweet syrup.
Arrange the apples and blueberries on top of each pastry square.

Bake in the preheated oven for 18–20 minutes, or until the pastry
is puffed and golden.

Serve warm with a little double cream spooned over the top.

rhubarb galette

250 g ready-made puff pastry, defrosted if frozen

4 tablespoons sugar

500 g rhubarb, cut into 5 cm lengths

50 g apricot jam, to glaze

crème fraîche, to serve

ground cinnamon, for dusting (optional)

serves 4–6

Impressive yet easy to make, this teatime galette doubles as a dessert. You can use apples or pears when rhubarb is out of season.

Take the pastry out of the fridge and let it rest for 20 minutes.

Preheat the oven to 200°C (400°F) Gas 6. Roll out the pastry into a 10 x 20 cm rectangle. Transfer to a baking tray and chill for 15 minutes.

Put the sugar in a saucepan with 120 ml water. Gently heat until the sugar dissolves, then increase the heat and boil for 1 minute until syrupy. Add the rhubarb pieces and cook for 5–7 minutes until just tender but not breaking up.

Remove with a slotted spoon and arrange in a single layer on the pastry, leaving a 5 mm edge of pastry uncovered. Discard the syrup. Bake in the preheated oven for 15–20 minutes until puffed and golden. Remove from the oven.

Put the apricot jam in a saucepan with 1 tablespoon water. Heat until the mixture begins to bubble, then brush over the rhubarb. Let cool, then serve with crème fraîche and a dusting of cinnamon, if using.

grape & lemon mascarpone tart

one 375-g sheet ready-rolled puff
pastry, defrosted if frozen

2 large eggs, separated

2 tablespoons caster sugar, plus
1 teaspoon for sprinkling

250-g tub mascarpone cheese

2½ tablespoons Limoncello
(Italian lemon liqueur)

250 g white seedless or halved and
seeded grapes, rinsed and dried

250 g red seedless or halved and
seeded grapes, rinsed and dried

1 teaspoon icing sugar

serves 6–8

This is a really simple summer dessert that you can make
with a ready-rolled pastry base. A gorgeous Italian lemon
liqueur gives a sharp edge to the creamy mascarpone.

Take the pastry out of the fridge and let it rest for 20 minutes.

Preheat the oven to 200°C (400°F) Gas 6. Unroll the pastry and lift
carefully onto a lightly greased baking tray. Trim around the edge to
make a 28-cm round.

Lightly whisk the egg whites and brush a thin layer onto the pastry.
Sprinkle with 1 teaspoon sugar, then use a fork to prick the pastry
all over. Bake in the preheated oven for 10–12 minutes until puffed
up and brown. Leave to cool while you make the topping.

Tip the mascarpone cheese into a bowl and gradually work in the
Limoncello. Using an electric hand-held whisk, beat the egg yolks
with the remaining caster sugar until pale, thick and creamy. Gently
fold the mascarpone mixture into the eggs until thoroughly blended.

Transfer the cooled pastry base to a large serving plate or tray.
Spread over the mascarpone mixture with a spatula, taking it almost
up to the edges. Scatter the grapes over the top.

Sift over the icing sugar and serve straight away, or chill the tart for
a couple of hours and sprinkle with icing sugar just before serving.

tarte au citron

1 recipe Sweet Tart Pastry
(page 42)

2 large eggs, plus 4 egg yolks

280 g caster sugar

finely grated zest of 2 unwaxed lemons

freshly squeezed juice of 5 lemons

250 ml double cream

4 tablespoons sour cream
or crème fraîche

4 tablespoons sifted icing sugar
or caster sugar, to glaze

pouring cream, to serve (optional)

a loose-based metal flan tin,
25–28 cm diameter,
4–5 cm deep

a cook's blowtorch (optional)

serves 8–10

This rich lemon tart is perhaps the most famous, and popular, of all French desserts. As with all classic recipes, many different versions abound, but this one get the balance right and ensures that the flavour of the eggs does not overwhelm the sharpness of the lemon.

Preheat the oven to 190°C (375°F) Gas 5.

Roll out the pastry thinly and use to line the flan tin. Bake blind following the method given on page 42. Reduce the oven temperature to 170°C (325°F) Gas 3.

Put the eggs and egg yolks in a bowl and beat well until thoroughly blended but not frothy. Beat in the sugar, followed by the lemon zest. Gradually beat in the lemon juice, followed by the double cream and sour cream.

Carefully pour the filling into the pastry case and bake in the preheated oven for 35–40 minutes. The centre of the tart should just wobble a little when the tart is pushed. Let cool on a wire rack in the tin. Remove the tart from the tin only when it is cool.

Dust with the icing sugar or caster sugar, then caramelize using a cook's blowtorch if you have one. Alternatively, protect the edge of the pastry with strips of foil and put the tart under a very hot preheated grill for 1–2 minutes until the sugar melts and browns (you may have to move the tart around to achieve an even colour). Let the tart cool and serve cold. Offer cream for pouring.

fresh raspberry tart

1 recipe Pâte Brisée (page 43)

2–3 tablespoons good-quality raspberry jam or preserve

600 ml double cream, or 300 ml double cream mixed with 300 ml crème fraîche

2 tablespoons framboise liqueur, (optional)

750 g fresh raspberries

150 ml raspberry or redcurrant jelly

a loose-based fluted tart tin, 20.5 cm diameter

serves 6–8

This deliciously summery tart celebrates the perfect marriage of raspberries and cream. It is simplicity itself to make, but must be assembled at the last moment to keep the freshness and crispness of the pastry.

Preheat the oven to 200°C (400°F) Gas 6.

Bring the pastry to room temperature. Roll out thinly on a lightly floured work surface and use to line the tart tin. Prick the base, chill or freeze for 15 minutes, then bake blind following the method given on page 12. Leave to cool.

Press the raspberry jam through a sieve to remove the seeds, then put into a large bowl. Add the cream and framboise, if using. Whisk until thick and just holding peaks. Spoon into the tart case and level the surface. Cover with the raspberries, arranging a final neat layer on top.

Put the raspberry jelly into a small saucepan and warm it gently until liquid. Brush over the raspberries to glaze. Put the tart into the fridge to chill and set for 10 minutes only before serving (no longer or the tart will go soggy).

variation You may like to brush the inside of the tart shell with melted white chocolate before filling and decorate the top with white chocolate curls to make it an extra special treat!

french apple tart

1 recipe Pâte Brisée (page 43)
4–5 dessert apples, peeled and cored
3 tablespoons caster sugar
50 g unsalted butter, cubed
4–6 tablespoons apricot jam
2 tablespoons Calvados
(apple brandy) or brandy
pouring cream, to serve (optional)

a loose-based tart tin,
25 cm diameter

serves 6–8

A French pâtisserie classic. The secret of this tart is patience and neatness because it just has to look beautiful! Make it with the juiciest apples you can find – Golden Delicious work very well.

Preheat the oven to 200°C (400°F) Gas 6 and put a baking tray in the oven to heat.

Bring the pastry to room temperature. Roll out thinly on a lightly floured work surface and use to line the tart tin. Chill or freeze for 15 minutes.

Meanwhile, slice the apples thinly, and coarsely chop up the uneven smaller pieces. Arrange these smaller pieces in the base of the tart. Cover with one-third of the slices any way you like. Arrange the remaining slices neatly in concentric rings over the chopped apples. Sprinkle with the sugar and dot with the butter.

Set the tart tin on the warmed baking tray and bake in the preheated oven for about 1 hour until the apples are very well browned and the pastry golden. Remove from the oven and transfer to a cooling rack. Wait for 5 minutes, then remove the tart tin.

Put the apricot jam and Calvados into a small saucepan and warm gently. Strain, then use to glaze the apples. Serve the tart at room temperature and offer cream for pouring.

tarte tatin

450 g ready-made puff pastry, defrosted if frozen

300 g granulated sugar

150 g chilled unsalted butter, thinly sliced

2¼–2½ kg evenly-sized dessert apples such as Cox's Orange Pippins, Golden Delicious or Jonagolds

crème fraîche or whipped cream, to serve

a flameproof tarte tatin tin or cast-iron frying pan, 28 cm diameter

serves 6

A tart named after the Tatin sisters who, as legend has it, created an upside-down apple tart by mistake! The type of apple used is crucial here – it must retain its shape during cooking and yet have a good flavour.

Roll out the pastry on baking parchment to a circle about 30 cm in diameter. Slide onto a baking tray and chill. Sprinkle the sugar over the base of the tarte tatin tin. Cover with the slices of butter.

Peel, halve and core the apples. Add the apple halves to the outside edge of the dish – set the first one at an angle, almost on its edge, then arrange the others all around the edge so that they slightly overlap and butt up against each other. Add another ring of apple slices inside, so that the tin is almost filled, then put a whole half to fill the gap in the centre.

Set the tin over gentle heat and cook for about 45 minutes until the sugar and butter have caramelized and the apples have softened underneath. The juices will gradually bubble up the sides; keep cooking until they are a dark amber.

Preheat the oven to 190°C (375°F) Gas 5.

Lay the pastry over the apples in the tin and tuck in the edges. Prick the top of the pastry with a fork, then set the tin on the baking tray. Bake in the preheated oven for 25–30 minutes until the pastry is risen and golden. Remove from the oven and invert the tart onto a warm serving plate. Serve warm with crème fraîche or cream.

mixed nut treacle tart

½ recipe Rich Shortcrust pastry
(page 45)

5 tablespoons treacle

5 tablespoons maple syrup

finely grated zest and juice of
1 unwaxed orange

100 g ground almonds

150 g mixed whole nuts such as
walnuts, hazelnuts, pecans, pine nuts
and almonds

custard, clotted cream or
crème fraîche, to serve

a deep tart tin, 20 cm diameter

serves 6

Incredibly rich and sticky, this tart can be packed with
whatever kinds of nuts you have available. Serve it as
a dessert, as here – or in small slices with coffee.

Preheat the oven to 190°C (375°F) Gas 5. Put a baking tray in to
heat up.

Roll out the pastry to a thickness of 5 mm. Use to line the tart tin,
trim and prick the base with a fork. Chill or freeze while you make
the filling.

Put the treacle, maple syrup, orange juice and zest in a saucepan
and heat until just warm and runny. Stir in the ground almonds.

Spread into the chilled or frozen pastry case and sprinkle the nuts
all over the surface. Transfer to the hot baking tray and bake in the
preheated oven for about 30 minutes or until the filling is just set
and the pastry is browning at the edges.

Remove from the oven and let cool slightly before serving warm with
custard, clotted cream or crème fraîche.

sweet tart pastry

180 g plain flour
a pinch of salt
40 g icing sugar
100 g unsalted butter, chilled
and cubed
1 large egg, separated
1½–2 tablespoons cold freshly
squeezed lemon juice or iced water

makes
sufficient to line a tart tin, 23–25 cm
or 6 tartlet tins, 9 cm diameter

This pastry is easily made in a food processor and creates a crisp, biscuity crust that is ideal for sweet tart cases. Don't be tempted to stint on the chilling – it makes the pastry much easier to roll out. Brushing the pastry with egg white as it cooks ensures a crisp finish and stops it becoming soggy.

Put the flour, salt, sugar and butter in a food processor fitted with metal blades. Process until the mixture has a sandy appearance. Add the egg yolk and 1½ tablespoons of the lemon juice and process again until the dough forms a ball and leaves the sides of the bowl. Add extra lemon juice or water if the dough seems dry and crumbly. Form the dough into a ball, wrap in foil and chill for 1 hour.

Remove from the fridge and let sit for 10–15 minutes at room temperature before rolling out. Put the dough on a lightly floured work surface and roll it out thinly. Use to line the tart tin, making sure you ease the dough into the corners of the tin without stretching it. Trim off the excess pastry.

To blind bake the tart case, take long, thin strips of foil and fold them over the edge of the tart, to protect and support the sides. Prick the base all over with a fork. Chill for 30–40 minutes.

Bake in a preheated oven at 190°C (375°F) Gas 5 for 8–10 minutes until lightly coloured. Beat the egg white with a fork to break it up. Remove the foil and brush the inside of the case with egg white. Return to the oven for another 8–10 minutes or until the pastry is golden brown and crisp. Let cool in the tin before using.

pâte brisée

200 g plain flour
a large pinch of salt
100 g unsalted butter, cubed, at room temperature
1 medium egg yolk
2½–3 tablespoons iced water

makes
sufficient to line a tart tin, 23–25 cm or 6 tartlet tins, 9 cm diameter

This pastry is the French version of an unsweetened shortcrust. It has a finer texture so should be rolled out much thinner – to about 3 mm. It is used for fruit tarts that are baked for a long time, because pastries with a high sugar content would scorch before the fruit was cooked.

Sift the flour and salt into a mound on a clean work surface. Make a well in the middle with your fist.

Put the butter and egg yolk into the well and using the fingers of one hand 'peck' the eggs and butter together until they resemble scrambled eggs.

Using a palette knife or pastry scraper, flick the flour over the egg mixture and chop through until almost amalgamated. Sprinkle with the water and chop again.

Bring together quickly with your hands. Knead lightly into a ball, then flatten slightly.

Wrap in clingfilm and chill for at least 30 minutes. Let it return to room temperature before rolling out.

american pie crust

375 g plain flour
a good pinch of salt
250 g white cooking fat, chilled
1 medium egg, beaten
1 tablespoon wine vinegar
or lemon juice
4 tablespoons iced water

makes
sufficient for 2 deep pie cases
or 1 lidded pie, 23–25 cm diameter

This is a recipe for the classic American pie crust. To give the crust a richer flavour and golden colour, unsalted butter can be substituted for the cooking fat, or you can use half butter and half cooking fat (or lard). It is a very light, crumbly pastry when baked – similar to shortcrust.

Sift the flour and salt into a large bowl. Cut in the fat using 2 round-bladed knives or do this in a food processor fitted with metal blades. Beat the egg in a separate bowl or jug. Stir in the vinegar or lemon juice, then add the water. Pour the wet mixture into the dry mixture, then cut it in with the knives or pastry blender again. Bring the dough together quickly using your hands.

Knead until smooth either in the bowl or on a floured work surface. Divide in 2 so it is easier to roll out later.

Shape the dough into flattened balls, wrap in clingfilm, then chill for at least 30 minutes before rolling out.

rich shortcrust pastry

250 g plain flour
½ teaspoon salt
125 g unsalted butter, chilled and cubed
2 medium egg yolks
2 tablespoons iced water

makes
sufficient to line a tart tin, 23–25 cm or 6 tartlet tins, 9 cm diameter

This is a wonderfully light and crumbly pastry. It is enriched with egg and made with butter only. It is best used for richer pies and tarts, or where the taste of the pastry is particularly important.

Sift the flour and salt together into a bowl, then rub in the butter. Mix the egg yolks with 2 tablespoons iced water. Add to the flour, mixing together lightly with a knife. (The pastry must have some water in it or it will be too difficult to handle. If it is still too dry, add a little more water, sprinkling it over the flour mixture 1 tablespoon at a time.)

Turn out the mixture onto a lightly floured work surface. Knead lightly with your hands until smooth, then form into a rough ball. Flatten slightly, then wrap in clingfilm and chill for at least 30 minutes before rolling out.

variation For a Sweet Shortcrust Pastry, sift 2 tablespoons icing sugar with the flour and salt.

crumbles, cobblers
& puddings

nectarine & ginger crumble

6 nectarines

75 ml apple juice

2 tablespoons finely chopped stem ginger

50 g caster sugar

100 g unsalted butter, melted

200 g ginger nuts or other ginger biscuits, crushed

100 g demerera sugar

vanilla ice cream or clotted cream, to serve

a medium, shallow ovenproof dish

serves 4

This is a useful recipe for when your nectarines are slightly hard, as cooking them softens the flesh and brings out the flavour. The topping is made with ginger-flavoured biscuits but you can substitute them with any crunchy biscuit and add a good pinch or two of ground ginger to the mixture.

Preheat the oven to 190°C (375°F) Gas 5. Put a baking tray on the middle shelf to heat.

Halve the nectarines and remove the stones, then slice or chop them. Tip them into an ovenproof baking dish and mix with the apple juice, chopped ginger and caster sugar.

To make the ginger topping, melt the butter in a saucepan and stir in the crushed biscuits and demerera sugar until the mixture resembles rough breadcrumbs.

Lightly sprinkle the topping mixture evenly over the surface of the nectarines, mounding it up a little towards the centre.

Place the baking dish on top of the baking tray in the preheated oven and bake for about 25 minutes, until crisp and golden on top.

Remove from the oven and let cool for 5 minutes before serving with vanilla ice cream or clotted cream.

toffee banana crumbles

8 bananas
50 g soft brown sugar
freshly squeezed juice of 1 lemon

for the coconut topping
50 g plain flour
50 g unsweetened desiccated coconut
50 g unsalted butter,
chilled and diced
25 g caster sugar
pouring cream, to serve

*4 individual heatproof
chef's presentation rings,
7 cm diameter*

serves 4

These little crumbles are a bit fiddly to make, but well worth the effort. Be very careful when transferring them from the pan to the plate – a fish slice will help. They make a spectacular dinner party dessert and a more sophisticated alternative to banoffi pie!

Preheat the oven to 190°C (375°F) Gas 5.

Trim and cut the bananas into 3-cm lengths. Reserve 4 lengths for the centres of the crumbles, then slice each of the remaining ones in half lengthways. Sprinkle the brown sugar into a heavy cast iron frying pan, then place 4 chef's rings into the sugar. Pack each ring with an upright banana. Next, tightly surround this with the split bananas (to resemble the petals of a flower) and pour the lemon juice over the bananas and sugar.

Now make the topping. Put the flour, coconut and butter into a food processor and process until it looks like coarse breadcrumbs. Alternatively you can rub in by hand. Tip into a bowl and stir in the sugar.

Fill each ring to the top with the coconut mixture. Place the frying pan in the preheated oven and bake for about 25 minutes, until golden. Remove from the oven and slip a fish slice under each ring and lift them out of the pan onto four warmed plates. Carefully remove the rings and serve warm with the remaining pan juices spooned around the crumbles. Offer a jug of cream for pouring.

raspberry, apple & almond crumble

3 large cooking apples, peeled, quartered, cored and sliced

3–4 tablespoons caster sugar

250 g fresh or frozen raspberries

crumble topping

150 g plain flour

25 g ground almonds

110 g butter, chilled and cubed

50 g caster sugar

25 g flaked almonds (optional)

vanilla ice cream or pouring cream, to serve

a shallow ovenproof dish, lightly greased

serves 6

The addition of raspberries to this otherwise traditional crumble not only gives it a gorgeous colour but creates a pleasing tartness.

Put the apples in a large saucepan. Sprinkle over 3 tablespoons sugar and add 3 tablespoons water. Cover the pan, place over low heat and cook for about 15 minutes, shaking the pan occasionally until the apple pieces are soft but still holding their shape. Stir in the raspberries and check for sweetness, adding a little extra sugar if it seems too sharp. Transfer to the prepared dish and let cool.

To make the topping, put the flour and ground almonds in a large bowl. Keep cutting the butter cubes into the flour mixture until you can't get the pieces of butter any smaller, then rub the butter and flour mixture together using your fingertips, until the mixture resembles coarse breadcrumbs. Stir in the sugar and carry on rubbing for another minute. Stir in the flaked almonds, if using.

When the fruit has cooled, preheat the oven to 200°C (400°F) Gas 6. Spread the crumble mixture evenly over the fruit, making sure you cover the whole surface. Bake in the preheated oven for about 35–40 minutes until the topping is golden and the fruit juices are bubbling around the sides of the dish. Leave to cool for 10–15 minutes before serving with vanilla ice cream or pouring cream.

rhubarb & apple crumble

2 cooking apples, peeled, cored
and sliced, about 400 g
250 g rhubarb, cut into chunks
4 tablespoons clear honey

crumble topping
40 g polyunsaturated margarine
125 g plain stoneground
wholemeal flour
75 g soft light brown sugar
40 g whole rolled oats
10 g whole almonds, chopped
pouring cream or yoghurt, to serve

a medium, shallow ovenproof dish

serves 6

Whole rolled oats, wholemeal flour and chopped almonds add a pleasingly crunchy texture to this crumble topping and with the margarine also make it a healthier choice than the more traditional flour and butter recipes.

Preheat the oven to 180°C (350°F) Gas 4.

Toss the fruit together with the honey in the baking dish. Sprinkle with 4 tablespoons of water, then cover with foil and bake in the preheated oven for 20 minutes.

Meanwhile, rub the margarine into the flour until the mixture resembles breadcrumbs. Stir in the sugar, oats and almonds.

When the fruit is ready, scatter the crumble mixture evenly over the top and press down gently. Return the dish to the oven and bake, uncovered, for 20 minutes until the topping is golden and the fruit juices are bubbling up around the edges.

Serve warm with pouring cream or yoghurt.

cranberry & orange streusel crisp

500 g fresh or frozen cranberries
finely grated zest and juice of
1 orange
clear honey, to taste
pouring cream, to serve

streusel topping
75 g plain flour
75 g soft brown sugar
75 g unsalted butter, chilled
and cubed

a small, shallow ovenproof dish

serves 4

This is really good made in individual dishes or cups, but make sure they are ovenproof. Serve each guest their own little jug of cold pouring cream so that they don't feel greedy reaching over the table for more!

Preheat the oven to 220°C (425°F) Gas 7.

Put the cranberries in a saucepan with the orange juice (not the zest) and bring to the boil. Cook for 2 minutes then remove from the heat and sweeten to taste with honey. Pour into a baking dish and let cool.

Mix the flour, sugar and orange zest in a bowl and add the cubes of butter. Rub the butter into the dry mixture until it resembles fine breadcrumbs and is on no account greasy or oily. Pop into a plastic bag and leave in the fridge for 20 minutes if it has become so.

Once the cranberries are cold, sprinkle evenly with the streusel topping and bake in the preheated oven for 10 minutes, then turn down the heat to 180°C (350°F) Gas 4 and bake for a further 15 minutes.

Remove from the oven and serve warm with pouring cream.

peach cobbler

6 peaches, not too ripe
1 tablespoon plain flour
1 tablespoon freshly squeezed lemon juice
3 tablespoons clear honey
pouring cream or vanilla ice cream, to serve

cobbler topping
125 ml double cream
5 tablespoons crème fraîche
165 g plain flour
50 g sugar, plus extra for sprinkling
1 teaspoon baking powder
¼ teaspoon bicarbonate of soda
a pinch of salt
50 g unsalted butter
2–3 tablespoons sugar, for sprinkling

a shallow ovenproof dish, about 2–2.5 litres

serves 6

This American classic should be eaten soon after baking because the cobbler dough soaks up the fruit juices upon standing. You can add a punnet of blackberries to the peaches, if you like, or use a combination of peaches, apricots and blackberries.

Preheat the oven to 190°C (375°F) Gas 5.

Cut the peaches in half, remove the stones, then cut each half into 3 slices, put them in the baking dish, sprinkle with the flour and toss well to coat evenly. Add the lemon juice and honey and stir. Set aside.

To make the topping, put the cream and crème fraîche in a large bowl and stir well. Set aside.

Put the flour, sugar, baking powder, bicarbonate of soda and salt in a large bowl and mix well. Add the butter and mix with your fingertips until the mixture resembles coarse breadcrumbs. Using a fork, stir in the cream mixture until blended – use your hands at the end if necessary, it should be sticky, thick and not willing to blend easily.

Drop spoonfuls of the mixture on top of the peaches, leaving gaps to expose the fruit. Sprinkle sugar liberally on top of the batter. Bake in the preheated oven for about 25–35 minutes, until golden. Serve warm with pouring cream or ice cream.

individual pear, maple & pecan cobblers

4 small ripe pears
finely grated zest and juice
of ½ lemon
4 tablespoons maple syrup
double cream or Greek-style yoghurt,
to serve

maple pecan cobbler topping
50 g unsalted butter,
chilled and cubed
225 g self-raising flour
a pinch of salt
3 tablespoons maple syrup
200 ml milk
50 g roughly chopped pecan nuts

a fluted 4–5 cm biscuit cutter
4 individual ovenproof ramekins
or similar

serves 4

These little individual cobblers will definitely impress as you bring them to the table. Use deep ramekins to achieve the starry effect. They look spectacular and taste just as good as they look.

Preheat the oven to 220°C (425°F) Gas 7.

Peel and core the pears, then slice them thickly lengthways (or quarter if small and thin). Put the pears into a saucepan with the lemon zest and juice and the maple syrup. Poach gently for 10 minutes until the fruit is almost tender. Set aside.

To make the topping, rub the butter into the flour and salt until it resembles fine breadcrumbs. Stir the maple syrup into the milk and add 150 ml to the flour, mixing with a blunt knife to form a fairly soft, sticky dough. Tip out onto a flour-dusted work surface, roll out until about 2 cm thick and stamp out 4 rounds with a biscuit cutter.

Take 4 ramekins and arrange the pear slices around the edge, with the thicker ends in the centre of the dish and the thinner ends pointing upwards out of the dishes as shown. Spoon the juice evenly over the pears and anchor them with a round of cobbler dough placed lightly in the centre. Brush each one with the remaining milk and sprinkle with chopped nuts. Place the ramekins on a baking tray.

Bake in the preheated oven for 10–15 minutes, until the dough is puffed golden brown, and the pears just browning at their tips. Serve hot with double cream or Greek-style yoghurt.

summer berry cobbler

900 g mixed summer berries
(raspberries, blueberries, small
strawberries, blackberries,
blackcurrants, cherries, etc)
3 tablespoons crème de cassis
(optional)
3 tablespoons sugar
pouring cream, to serve

lemon cobbler topping
50 g unsalted butter, chilled
225 g self-raising flour
a pinch of salt
75 g caster sugar
finely grated zest of 2 unwaxed lemons
150 ml milk
freshly squeezed juice of 1 lemon

a medium, shallow ovenproof dish

serves 4–6

This deliciously fruity cobbler is covered with tiny lemon-flavoured dumplings. You can use whatever fresh berries are in season and frozen mixed berries work well too.

Preheat the oven to 200°C (400°F) Gas 6.

Pick over the berries, discarding any really soft or bruised fruits. Mix them with the crème de cassis (if using) and sugar and pour into an ovenproof baking dish.

Rub the butter into the flour and salt until it resembles fine breadcrumbs. Stir in 50 g of the sugar and the lemon zest. Add the milk to the flour, mixing with a blunt knife to a fairly soft, sticky dough. Tip out onto a flour-dusted work surface and knead lightly. Roll into a long thin sausage and using sharp scissors, snip off little hazelnut-sized pieces. Scatter these lightly over the berries.

Mix the lemon juice with the remaining sugar and liberally brush all over the 'dumplings'.

Bake in the preheated oven for 15 minutes, until the pastry is golden brown and the fruit softened and bubbling. Remove from the oven and serve hot with pouring cream.

apricot & almond slump

600 g fresh apricots
100 g unrefined caster sugar
vanilla ice cream, to serve

almond slump batter
200 g plain flour
3 teaspoons baking powder
a pinch of salt
50 g unrefined caster sugar
100 g ground almonds
350 ml milk
50 g unsalted butter, melted
30 g whole blanched almonds

a large, non-stick, metal baking tin, lightly buttered

serves 4–6

Slump perfectly describes the sloppy batter which covers the seasonal fruit in this satisfying pudding. You can use any juicy summer fruit and berries are good too. If liked, you can substitute pine nuts for the almonds. Simply sprinkle them all over the batter.

Preheat the oven to 190°C (375°F) Gas 5.

Halve the apricots, remove the stones and mix with 100 g of the sugar. Set aside until needed.

Sift together the flour and baking powder and add the salt and sugar to the bowl. Stir in the ground almonds, the milk and melted butter and whisk until smooth and thick. Pour the batter into the prepared tin, then push in the apricots cut-side up, but in a higgledy-piggledy manner and slightly at an angle all over. Place a whole almond inside each apricot where the stone once was.

Bake in the middle of the preheated oven for 25–30 minutes, until risen and golden.

Remove from the oven and let cool slightly before serving with vanilla ice cream.

orange & sultana pudding with cardamom

6 cardamom pods

60 g caster sugar

2 eggs, separated, plus
2 extra egg whites

grated zest of ½ unwaxed orange, plus
freshly squeezed juice of 1 orange

250 g Quark cheese

50 g self-raising stoneground
wholemeal flour

a pinch of salt

50 g sultanas

sauce

3 tablespoons clear honey

grated zest of ½ unwaxed orange,
plus freshly squeezed juice of 1 orange

freshly squeezed juice of ½ lemon

1 rounded tablespoon arrowroot
or cornflour

250 ml boiling water

*a 1.2-litre shallow ovenproof dish,
lightly greased*

a large roasting tin

serves 6

This hot pudding has a lovely light texture and is a cross between a steamed sponge pudding and a soufflé. Perfect for a chilly winter day.

Preheat the oven to 180°C (350°F) Gas 4. Sit the baking dish inside the roasting tin.

Put the cardamom pods in a mortar and crush with a pestle to extract the seeds. Discard the papery husks and grind the seeds to a powder. Tip into a mixing bowl, add the sugar, egg yolks and orange zest, then whisk for 2 minutes using an electric mixer until pale, frothy and thickened.

Whisk the Quark and orange juice into the egg mixture until smooth, then sift in the flour and salt. Tip in any bran left in the sieve, then stir in, followed by the sultanas.

In a separate bowl, and using clean whisks, beat the 4 egg whites until soft peaks form. Stir a spoonful into the batter to loosen the mixture, then carefully but quickly fold in the remainder. Pour into the prepared baking dish inside the roasting tin. Pour boiling water into the roasting tin to come halfway up the sides of the baking dish. Bake in the preheated oven for 25 minutes until the pudding is golden brown and well risen.

Meanwhile, to make the sauce, put the honey, orange zest and juice and lemon juice in a small saucepan. Blend in the arrowroot or cornflour until smooth, then mix in the boiling water. Bring to the boil, stirring until thickened. Serve the hot sauce poured over each serving of pudding.

steamed syrup pudding

250 g unsalted butter, softened
250 g caster sugar
3 eggs
375 g self-raising flour
50 ml milk
4 tablespoons golden syrup
vanilla ice cream, to serve

a pudding basin, 1 litre capacity, well buttered

serves 4

An easy-to-make winter classic, this pudding is always a winner. You could omit the syrup and use the same volume of honey, jam, lemon curd or a little chopped stem ginger.

Put the butter and sugar in a medium mixing bowl and beat with a wooden spoon until pale and creamy. Add the eggs one at a time and beat until blended.

Sift the flour over the egg mixture and fold in. Add the milk and continue folding the mixture until smooth.

Pour the golden syrup into the buttered pudding basin. Spoon the sponge mixture on top. Cover with baking parchment and secure with kitchen string.

Sit the pudding basin in a large saucepan. Pour in boiling water from the kettle until it comes about halfway up the sides of the basin. Cover and simmer gently for 1 hour, topping up with more boiling water as necessary.

Carefully remove the pudding basin from the saucepan and peel off the paper. Place a large serving plate on top of the basin, then turn the pudding over, giving it a gentle shake to release it from the mould.

Cut the pudding into slices at the table and serve with ice cream.

warm chocolate pudding

1 teaspoon instant coffee granules
175 g unsalted butter
175 g unrefined caster sugar
2 large eggs
225 g self-raising flour
50 g cocoa powder
pouring cream, to serve

chocolate sauce
100 g dark chocolate
(minimum 70% cocoa solids),
broken into pieces
100 g unsalted butter
50 g unrefined caster sugar
200 ml double cream

*a pudding basin, 1 litre capacity,
well buttered*

serves 8

This pudding can be made in advance, then just reheated on the day. Don't scrimp on the chocolate sauce ingredients: they make a thick, rich and glossy sauce that will become one of your favourites.

Put the coffee into a small cup, add 1 teaspoon of boiling water and stir to dissolve. Put 10 cm water into a saucepan large enough to hold the pudding basin. Put the butter and sugar into a bowl and, using an electric whisk, beat until creamy, light and very pale. Add the eggs and coffee and beat again.

Sift in the flour and cocoa powder and fold with a large metal spoon, adding a little milk if the mixture seems very stiff. Transfer to the prepared pudding basin and cover tightly with buttered foil or baking parchment. Put into the saucepan of water, cover with a lid and bring to the boil. Reduce the heat and simmer for 1½ hours, checking the water level from time to time.

Meanwhile make the sauce. Put the chocolate, butter, sugar and cream into a small saucepan. Heat gently, stirring frequently, until melted. Remove from the heat and set aside until ready to serve.

Remove the bowl from the saucepan and carefully turn out the pudding onto a large serving plate. Serve hot or warm with the chocolate sauce and cream for pouring.

sticky toffee puddings

80 ml dulce de leche
115 g unsalted butter,
at room temperature
115 g sugar
2 eggs
115 g self-raising flour
40 g walnut pieces
double cream or vanilla ice cream,
to serve

*six 150-ml individual pudding
moulds or a pudding basin, buttered*

serves 6

What makes this recipe a real winner is the dulce de leche, a soft, buttery toffee sauce that can now be found in most large supermarkets. If you can't find it, make it by boiling an unopened can of condensed milk in a pan of water for about 3 hours, then let it cool before opening.

Pour or spoon the dulce de leche into the bottom of the prepared pudding moulds or basin.

Beat together the butter and sugar until pale and creamy, then beat in the eggs, one at a time. Sift over the flour and fold in, then stir in the walnuts. Pour the mixture into the moulds or basin.

Cover each pudding with 2 sheets of foil and tie firmly in place with a piece of kitchen string.

Put the puddings in a large pan and pour boiling water into the pan about two-thirds of the way up the sides of the puddings. Cover with a lid and simmer gently for about 1½ hours, checking the water level occasionally and topping up if necessary.

To serve, remove the foil, invert the puddings onto serving plates, and lift off. Serve warm with double cream or ice cream.

baked lemon pudding

50 g unsalted butter
285 g caster sugar
3 eggs, separated
3 tablespoons self-raising flour
375 ml milk
65 ml freshly squeezed lemon juice
1 tablespoon icing sugar

a medium, ovenproof baking dish

serves 6

This is perfect for lovers of tangy yet comforting desserts. Meyer lemons are ideal because they have a thin skin and juicy pulp making them perfect for juicing and cooking. But actually this will taste good whichever lemons you use!

Preheat the oven to 180°C (350°F) Gas 4.

Put the butter and sugar in a food processor and process for about 10 seconds, until smooth. Add the egg yolks one at a time to the mixture and process for a few seconds after each addition.

Add the flour and process until smooth. With the motor running pour in the milk in a slow and steady stream, scraping down the bowl of the food processer with a spatula so all the mixture is incorporated and lump free. Transfer the mixture to a large bowl.

Using a hand-held electric whisk, beat the egg whites until firm, then fold them into the batter in two batches using a large metal spoon. Quickly stir in the lemon juice. Spoon the mixture into the baking dish and bake in the preheated oven for 25–30 minutes, until golden on top.

Let the pudding rest for 10 minutes before dusting with icing sugar to serve.

note: v. nice took longer to cook & Golden only @ edges — ? try top oven or gas 5.

bread & butter puddings

300 ml milk
300 ml double cream
½ teaspoon vanilla extract
4 tablespoons caster sugar
3 eggs
6 tea cakes or hot cross buns, halved
50 g sultanas
freshly grated nutmeg, to taste
pouring cream, to serve (optional)

*six 200-ml individual ramekins,
well buttered*

serves 6

Bread and butter pudding is a comfort classic and many people's childhood favourite. This version updates a wonderfully retro recipe slightly as you make them in individual dishes that will cook in under 20 minutes.

Put the milk, cream, vanilla extract and 3 tablespoons of the sugar into a saucepan and heat until the sugar dissolves.

Put the eggs into a bowl, whisk well, stir in 2–3 tablespoons of the hot milk mixture just to warm the eggs, then stir in the remainder of the hot milk.

Preheated the oven to 180°C (350°F) Gas 4.

Lightly toast the tea cakes or hot cross buns and cut them into quarters. Divide the pieces between the 6 prepared ramekins and sprinkle with the sultanas.

Pour in the custard mixture, grate a little nutmeg over the top and sprinkle with the remaining sugar.

Bake in the preheated oven for 18–20 minutes until firm. Let cool a little, then serve warm with cream, if liked.

rice pudding

125 g risotto rice, such as arborio
500 ml full-fat milk, boiled
60 g sugar
1 vanilla pod, split lengthways
15 g unsalted butter
a pinch of salt
fruit purée, jam or chocolate sauce,
to serve (optional)

serves 4

Here is a very simple, classic recipe for this popular comfort food. Cooking the rice twice blanches it first and removes much of the starch. The result is light and delicate, not blobby and glutinous as some rice puddings can be.

Put the rice in a saucepan with a lid and add cold water to cover. Slowly bring to the boil over medium heat, then boil for 5 minutes. Drain the rice and rinse under cold water. Set aside to drain well.

Meanwhile, put the milk in an ovenproof pan with a lid and bring to the boil. Add the sugar and vanilla pod. Remove from the heat, cover and let stand for 15 minutes. Using the tip of the knife, scrape out the vanilla seeds and stir them through the milk.

Preheat the oven to 180°C (350°F) Gas 4.

Add the drained rice to the milk, then add the butter and salt. Bring slowly to the boil. Cover and transfer to the preheated oven. Do not stir. Let cook for about 25–35 minutes, until the rice is tender and the liquid is almost completely absorbed but not dry.

Serve warm with a swirl of fruit purée, jam or chocolate sauce if liked.

cherry & almond clafoutis

100 g blanched almonds
1 vanilla pod (optional)
3 tablespoons plain flour
225 g caster sugar
4 eggs
2 egg yolks
250 ml single cream
250 g cherries, torn in half and stoned
vanilla ice cream, to serve

*a round, ovenproof dish
20–23 cm diameter*

serves 4

Traditionally, the fruit baked in this classic French dessert were the first cherries of the season, although this recipe would make an equally lovely pudding using other stone fruits such as small peaches, nectarines or apricots.

Preheat the oven to 220°C (425°F) Gas 7.

Put the almonds on a baking tray and toast them in the preheated oven for 6–8 minutes, until lightly golden. Remove and let cool. Put the cooled almonds in a food processor and process until they resemble breadcrumbs. Scrape the seeds from the vanilla pod, if using, into the food processor with the almonds and process a second time. Add the flour and sugar and process to mix. Add the eggs, egg yolks and cream and process again until you have a smooth, thick batter. Transfer to a bowl, cover and chill until needed. This mixture will keep for 2 days in the fridge.

Put the torn cherry halves in the bottom of the ovenproof dish. Carefully pour the batter over the cherries. If need be, rearrange the cherries to evenly distribute. (If using chilled batter, beat it until well mixed before pouring over the cherries.)

Bake in the preheated oven for 25 minutes, until the clafoutis is puffed up and golden brown. Let cool for a few minutes before serving. The clafoutis will sink during this time.

Serve hot with vanilla ice cream.

fig & honey croissant pudding

2 croissants, preferably stale,
each torn into 6 pieces
6 fresh figs, halved
60 ml honey
3 eggs
250 ml full-fat milk
250 ml single cream
55 g caster sugar
double cream, to serve

*a medium ovenproof dish,
lightly greased*

serves 4

Fresh figs have a sweet, honey-nectar flavour. Once picked, they ripen very quickly and late-season figs are perfect cooked in puddings like this quick and easy recipe.

Preheat the oven to 180°C (350°F) Gas 4.

Put the croissant pieces in the bottom of the greased dish. Arrange the fig halves in between the croissant pieces and drizzle the honey over the top.

Combine the eggs, milk, cream and sugar in a bowl and pour into the dish. Let stand for about 20 minutes so that the croissants can absorb some of the custard. Bake in the preheated oven for 50 minutes, until the top of the pudding is a dark golden brown.

Let cool a little before cutting into slices and serving with dollops of double cream on the side.

variation When figs aren't available, you can lightly spread each piece of croissant with some good-quality fig jam before putting into the dish. Leave out the honey and add 60 g slivered almonds to the egg mixture instead.

summer pudding

500 g fresh or frozen berries, such as raspberries, blackberries, small strawberries or mixed summer berries, defrosted, if frozen

2 tablespoons clear honey

125 ml red wine

1 cinnamon stick, bruised

8 slices white or multigrain day-old bread, crusts removed

1 teaspoon arrowroot

crème fraîche or yoghurt, to serve

a pudding basin or mould, 475 ml capacity

serves 4

Now that frozen summer fruits are readily available you can enjoy this quintessentially summery dessert all year round. For best results, chill the pudding in the fridge overnight.

If you are using fresh fruit, lightly rinse and let dry. Put the berries, honey, red wine, 125 ml water and cinnamon stick in a medium saucepan and gently simmer over low heat for 5 minutes, until the berries are plump and slightly softened. Remove from the heat and let cool. Discard the cinnamon stick.

Cut 6 slices of bread into triangles and use them to line the base and sides of the basin or mould. Overlap the bread so it completely covers the basin, leaving no gaps. Reserve the remaining 2 slices of bread to cover the top of the pudding. Spoon a little of the berry juice evenly over the bread in the basin to moisten it. Fill the bowl with the berries, using a slotted spoon and reserve any remaining berry juice. Pack the fruit down with the back of a spoon, taking care not to squash it too much. Slice the remaining bread into triangles. Put these on top of the fruit to make a 'lid'.

Cover the basin with clingfilm, put a small plate on top, then put weights on the plate to press it down onto the pudding. Chill in the fridge overnight then remove the weights, plate and clingfilm. Carefully invert the pudding onto a plate and remove the basin.

Put the reserved juice in a saucepan and heat gently. Blend the arrowroot with 1 tablespoon water and stir into the hot juice. Stir until the juice thickens and clears. Pour the sauce over the pudding. Serve with crème fraîche or yoghurt.

cakes & cheesecakes

almond & blood orange syrup cake

250 g blanched almonds

225 g caster sugar

50 g self-raising flour

250 g unsalted butter, at room temperature

1 tablespoon finely grated blood orange zest

4 eggs

60 g flaked almonds, lightly toasted

extra thick double cream, to serve

blood orange syrup

65 ml freshly squeezed blood orange juice

55 g caster sugar

a springform cake tin, 22 cm diameter, lightly greased

serves 8

Blood oranges have a sherbety orange flavour with hints of raspberry and a great colour. The fact that they are a truly seasonal fruit, available only for a few months from late autumn, makes them even more special to cook with and they make all the difference to this deliciously sticky cake.

Preheat the oven to 180°C (350°F) Gas 4.

Put the almonds in a food processor and process until finely chopped. Transfer them to a bowl and mix in the sugar and flour.

Beat the butter and zest for 1 minute, then add the eggs, one at a time, beating well after each addition until well mixed. Add the almond and flour mixture in 2 batches and beat again until well combined. Spoon into the prepared cake tin. Bake in the preheated oven for 45 minutes, until golden on top. Remove the cake from the oven and prick it all over with a skewer.

To make the syrup, put the blood orange juice and sugar in a small saucepan set over high heat, stirring until the sugar has dissolved. As soon as the mixture boils remove the pan from the heat and pour the syrup over the cake.

Let the cake cool in the tin then sprinkle the flaked almonds on top. Cut into slices and serve with extra thick double cream on the side.

lemon polenta cake

175 g unsalted butter, softened

175 g unrefined caster sugar

100 g polenta

½ teaspoon baking powder

175 g ground almonds

finely grated zest and juice of
1 unwaxed lemon

½ teaspoon vanilla extract

3 eggs

crème fraîche, to serve

syrup

finely grated zest and juice of
2 unwaxed lemons

50 g unrefined caster sugar

*a springform cake tin, 24 cm
diameter, lightly greased*

Polenta (Italian cornmeal) gives a coarser and grainier texture to a cake than wheat flour, but it is still delicious.

Preheat the oven to 180°C (350°F) Gas 4.

Beat together the butter and sugar until creamy. Add the polenta, baking powder, ground almonds, lemon zest and juice, vanilla extract and eggs. Mix together until smooth. Spoon the mixture into the prepared tin and bake in the middle of the preheated oven for 30 minutes.

Meanwhile, make the syrup. Put the lemon zest and juice in a small saucepan with the icing sugar and 2 tablespoons of water. Set over medium heat and bring to the boil. Let simmer for 2 minutes.

When the cake is done, let cool slightly in the tin, then turn out and pierce all over with a skewer. Spoon the syrup over the cake and then let stand for 20 minutes while it is absorbed.

Serve with a dollop of crème fraîche on the side.

peach & raspberry scone cake

375 g self-raising flour
500 ml whipping cream
250 ml clear, fizzy lemonade
100 g good-quality raspberry jam
2 peaches, stoned and sliced
1 punnet fresh raspberries

a loose-based fluted tart tin,
20 cm diameter, lightly greased

serves 8

Somewhere between an American shortcake and a scone, this cake is easy and delicious. Because the method is so simple the final result is largely dependent on the quality of the fruit used, so do choose good, firm and still fragrant peaches and freshly-picked raspberries if possible.

Preheat the oven to 180°C (350°F) Gas 4.

Put the flour in a large bowl and make a well in the centre. Add half of the cream and the lemonade and use a wooden spoon to mix together.

Spoon the mixture into the prepared tin, gently pressing down to fit, and bake in the preheated oven for 30–35 minutes, until golden brown on top. Remove the cake from the oven and let cool.

Using a long, sharp knife, slice about 0.5 cm off the top of the cake to create an even surface. Spread the jam evenly over the top of the cake.

Whip the remaining cream until soft peaks form. Spoon the cream on top of the cake and arrange the fruit in an attractive way on top. Keep chilled in the fridge until ready to serve.

strawberry buttermilk cake

250 g self-raising flour
225 g caster sugar
125 g unsalted butter, softened
2 eggs
225 g buttermilk
375 g strawberries, hulled, large ones halved
custard or double cream, to serve

crumble topping
40 g plain flour
50 g unsalted butter, chilled and cubed
95 g soft brown sugar

a cake tin, 24 x 24 cm square, greased and lined

serves 6–8

This smooth, dense cake has a light and creamy crumb and is simplicity itself to make in a food processor.

Preheat the oven to 180°C (350°F) Gas 4.

Combine the flour and sugar. Put the butter, eggs and buttermilk in a food processor and process until combined and smooth. With the motor running, add the flour and sugar mixture and process until well mixed. Scrape down the sides of the processor bowl to evenly incorporate all the ingredients and then stir in the strawberries. Spoon or pour the batter into the prepared cake tin.

To make the crumble topping, put the flour and butter in a bowl and, using your fingertips, rub the butter into the flour until the mixture resembles coarse breadcrumbs. Stir in the sugar.

Evenly sprinkle the topping mixture over the cake and bake in the preheated oven for 50 minutes, until golden brown on top.

Let cool before cutting into squares and serving with hot custard or a dollop of double cream on the side.

mocha fudge cake

175 g unsalted butter

275 g dark chocolate, broken into pieces

250 g caster sugar

3 large eggs

100 g plain flour

2 tablespoons instant coffee granules dissolved in 2 tablespoons just-boiled water

icing sugar, to dust

double cream, to serve (optional)

a round cake tin, 20 cm diameter, greased and base-lined

serves 8

The bitter coffee in this delicious dessert cake takes the edge off the sweetness of the chocolate. The outer crust bakes to a crisp yet still moist firmness, while the centre is meltingly soft. Serve with a fork and a dollop of double cream if you're feeling particularly indulgent.

Preheat the oven to 160°C (325°F) Gas 3.

Put the butter and chocolate in a heatproof bowl set over a saucepan of simmering water. Heat gently, stirring, until melted. Make sure the bowl does not touch the water. Remove from the heat and let cool for 5 minutes.

Stir in the sugar, then beat in the eggs, one at a time. Sift over the flour and fold in, then stir in the coffee.

Tip the mixture into the prepared cake tin and bake in the preheated oven for about 55 minutes, until firm to the touch and pale and speckled on top. (There should be a slight wobble in the centre, but the cake will firm up as it cools.) Remove from the oven and let cool in the tin.

To serve, carefully remove the cake from the pan and put on a serving plate. Dust with icing sugar, cut into wedges and serve with double cream, if liked.

chocolate & blackberry roulade

110 g caster sugar

2 large eggs

50 g unsalted butter, very soft

100 g self-raising flour

3 tablespoons cocoa powder

1 teaspoon vanilla extract

icing sugar, for dusting

chocolate curls or grated chocolate

cream filling

4 tablespoons blackberry conserve

200 g crème fraîche

250 g fresh blackberries, picked over to clean

a Swiss roll tin, 20 x 30 cm, buttered and lined with non-stick baking parchment

serves 6–8

A great stand-by pudding for a special dinner when time is tight. The roulade is a simple all-in-one cake mix, baked in 8 minutes and filled with crème fraîche mixed with conserve and fresh berries.

Preheat the oven to 200°C (400°F) Gas 6.

Put the sugar, eggs and butter in a mixing bowl. Sift the flour and cocoa into the bowl, then add the vanilla extract and 2 tablespoons warm water. Whisk until you have a smooth and thick cake batter.

Pour the mixture into the prepared Swiss roll tin and spread it evenly with a spatula. Bake in the preheated oven for about 8 minutes, or until the mixture is well risen and just springy when lightly pressed. Let cool in the tin for 1 minute.

Put a sheet of non-stick baking parchment on a work surface and sprinkle heavily with icing sugar. Turn the sponge out onto the baking parchment, then peel off the lining paper. Carefully roll up the sponge with the parchment inside. Cover with a damp tea towel and leave on the wire rack until completely cold.

To make the filling, put the conserve and creme fraiche into a bowl and, using a metal spoon, fold gently together. Carefully unroll the sponge. Spread the cream mixture over the sponge. Sprinkle the berries evenly over the top. Roll up the sponge and set on a serving plate. Cover and chill until ready to serve. Just before serving, dust with icing sugar and decorate with chocolate curls.

variation The roulade can also be made with raspberries, strawberries, blueberries or dark cherries (stoned) all with their matching conserves.

hazelnut roulade

6 eggs
175 g caster sugar,
plus extra for sprinkling
50 g self-raising flour, sifted
75 g hazelnuts,
toasted and finely ground
1 tablespoon unsalted butter, melted
icing sugar, for dusting

filling
200 ml Greek-style yoghurt
125 g raspberries

*a Swiss roll tin, about 20 x 30 cm,
buttered and lined with
non-stick baking parchment*

serves 6–8

The lightest and airiest of sponges, rolled with a filling of creamy Greek-style yoghurt and raspberries.

Preheat the oven to 200°C (400°F) Gas 6.

Put the eggs and sugar in a mixing bowl and whisk until pale, thick and creamy. The mixture should leave a ribbon-like trail on the surface when lifted.

Using a large metal spoon, fold in the flour and hazelnuts. Drizzle the melted butter over the surface of the mixture, then fold it in carefully.

Pour the mixture into the prepared Swiss roll tin and level the surface with a spatula. Bake in the preheated oven for about 15–20 minutes, until golden and the sponge springs back when lightly pressed.

Remove from the oven and turn out onto non-stick parchment paper sprinkled with caster sugar. Peel off the lining paper and trim the edges of the roulade. Roll up the sponge from the short end with the paper inside. Cover with a damp tea towel and leave on a wire rack until completely cold.

When ready to fill, gently unroll the sponge and remove the paper. Spread with a layer of yoghurt and add the raspberries. Roll up and set on a large serving plate. Cover and chill until ready to serve. Just before serving, dust with icing sugar.

black forest gâteau

chocolate sponge
9 large eggs, separated
200 g caster sugar
90 g cocoa powder, sifted

cherry filling
720-g jar or tin Morello cherries
in syrup
3 tablespoons kirsch
(a 50 ml miniature bottle)
425 ml double or whipping cream
3 tablespoons caster sugar
55 g dark chocolate, grated

*3 sandwich tins, 20 cm diameter,
buttered and base-lined*

serves 8–10

This traditional German recipe is nothing like the commercial cakes on sale these days – this is the real thing!

Preheat the oven to 180°C (350°F) Gas 4.

Put the egg yolks and sugar into a mixing bowl and whisk until very thick and mousse-like. Sift the cocoa onto the mixture and gently fold in with a large metal spoon.

Put the egg whites into a grease-free bowl and whisk until stiff peaks form. Carefully fold into the yolk mixture in 3 batches. Divide the mixture between the 3 prepared tins. Bake in the preheated oven for 20–25 minutes, until the sponge cakes spring back when lightly pressed. Let cool in the tins before turning out onto a wire rack and peeling off the lining paper.

Drain the cherries in a sieve and save the syrup – you will need about 4 tablespoons. When the cherries have been well drained, leave them on kitchen paper. Select 12 to decorate. Add the kirsch to the reserved syrup. Set one of the cooled sponges onto a serving plate, then drizzle with 2 tablespoons of the kirsch-flavoured syrup.

Put the cream into a bowl and whip until soft peaks form. Sprinkle the sugar over the cream and whip until slightly thicker. Set aside half the cream to cover the cake. Spread half the remaining cream onto the bottom layer of sponge. Press half the cherries into the cream. Sprinkle the second sponge layer with the kirsch syrup as before, then gently set on top of the first layer. Spread with cream and press in the cherries as before. Top with the final layer of sponge. Sprinkle with the remaining kirsch syrup. Cover the top and sides of the cake with the rest of the cream then decorate with the reserved cherries and grated chocolate. Chill until ready to serve.

italian chocolate amaretto torta

110 g dark chocolate, chopped

2 tablespoons Amaretto liqueur

110 g unsalted butter,
at room temperature

110 g caster sugar, plus 1 tablespoon

3 large eggs, separated

60 g amaretti biscuits, crushed

60 g plain flour, sifted

whipped cream, to serve

blueberries or raspberries,
to serve (optional)

*a loose-based sandwich tin,
20 cm diameter, buttered,
base-lined and floured*

serves 8

A delicious finale for a lovely summertime dinner, serve this very light cake with piles of berries and whipped cream.

Preheat the oven to 180°C (350°F) Gas 4.

Put the chocolate and Amaretto into a heatproof bowl set over a saucepan of steaming but not boiling water and leave until melted (do not let the base of the bowl touch the water). Remove the bowl from the heat, stir gently and let cool.

Put the butter and the 110 g caster sugar into a mixing bowl and beat until very light and fluffy. Beat in the egg yolks one at a time, then stir in the cooled melted chocolate. When thoroughly blended, use a large metal spoon to fold in the crushed biscuits and flour.

Put the egg whites into a grease-free bowl and whisk until stiff peaks form. Whisk in the remaining 1 tablespoon sugar to make a stiff, glossy meringue, then fold into the cake mixture in 3 batches.

Transfer the mixture to the prepared tin and bake in the preheated oven for 30–35 minutes, until just firm to the touch. Let cool in the tin for 10 minutes. Remove from the tin and transfer to a wire rack to cool completely.

Sprinkle with icing sugar and serve slightly warm or at room temperature with whipped cream and fresh berries.

praline profiteroles with sticky coffee sauce

115 g plain flour
90 ml milk
75 g unsalted butter, cubed
3 eggs

coffee sauce
140 g white chocolate, broken into pieces
60 ml double cream
60 ml freshly brewed espresso
1 tablespoon Kahlúa or other coffee liqueur

praline cream
5 tablespoons caster sugar
60 g blanched hazelnuts
240 ml double cream

2 baking trays, lined with parchment paper

serves 4

Nothing beats the pure indulgence of these light pastry puffs filled with a praline cream and drenched in a rich, sticky coffee and white chocolate sauce.

To make the coffee sauce, put the chocolate, cream, espresso and Kahlúa in a saucepan and heat gently, stirring, until smooth and creamy. Pour into a small jug and chill.

To make the praline, gently heat the sugar in a dry saucepan, stirring, for about 5 minutes until melted and golden. Add the hazelnuts and cook, stirring constantly, for about 1 minute, then tip onto a sheet of parchment paper and let cool.

Preheat the oven to 220°C (425°F) Gas 7.

Sift the flour onto a sheet of parchment paper and set aside. Put the milk, butter and 90 ml water in a large saucepan and bring to the boil. Remove from the heat, tip in the flour and beat until smooth. Return to the heat, stirring constantly, for 1 minute, then remove from the heat. Beat in the eggs, one at a time, until the mixture is smooth and glossy.

Drop neat spoonfuls of the mixture onto the prepared baking trays, spacing well apart, to make 12 buns. Bake in the preheated oven for about 20 minutes until risen and crisp. Transfer to a wire rack, cut a slit in the side of each one to release the steam, and let cool.

To serve, put the praline in a food processor and grind to a powder. Whip the cream and fold in the praline, then fill the profiteroles with the cream using a teaspoon. Pour over the coffee sauce and serve.

cappuccino cheesecake

150 g dark chocolate-covered digestives or other wheaten biscuits

60 g unsalted butter, melted

500 g mascarpone

125 ml crème fraîche

3 tablespoons instant coffee granules, dissolved in 3 tablespoons just-boiled water

125 g caster sugar, plus 1½ tablespoons for the topping

4 whole eggs plus 1 egg yolk, beaten together

240 ml sour cream

cocoa powder, to dust

a springform cake tin, 20 cm diameter, greased

a large roasting tin

serves 8

This smooth, creamy mascarpone cheesecake is topped with a layer of sour cream and dusted with cocoa, so that a slice really does resemble a cup of cappuccino.

Put the biscuits in a food processor and process until they become crumbs, then combine with the melted butter. Tip the mixture into the prepared cake tin. Smooth out and press down to make an even crust. Cover and chill for 30 minutes.

Preheat the oven to 180°C (350°F) Gas 4.

Beat together the mascarpone and crème fraîche until smooth, then stir in the coffee and sugar. Beat in the eggs until well combined.

Wrap the base and sides of the tin in two single sheets of foil, then pour the mascarpone mixture over the crumb crust. Put in a roasting tin and pour water around the cake tin so that it reaches half to two-thirds of the way up the sides. Bake in the preheated oven for about 50 minutes, until set but still soft.

Meanwhile, stir the remaining 1½ tablespoons sugar into the sour cream. Remove the cheesecake from the oven, gently spoon over the sour cream, spreading it out evenly, then return to the hot oven for 10 minutes.

Remove from the oven and let cool, then cover and chill for at least 4 hours or overnight. When ready to serve, carefully remove from the cake tin and dust with cocoa powder.

blueberry cheesecake

50 g unsalted butter

110 g digestive or other wheaten biscuits, crushed into fine crumbs

50–75 g caster sugar

250 g blueberries

1 teaspoon arrowroot

first layer

two 200-g tubs full-fat cream cheese

2 large eggs

100 g caster sugar

¼ teaspoon vanilla extract

second layer

284-ml carton soured cream

150 ml Greek-style yoghurt

2½ tablespoons caster sugar

1 teaspoon vanilla extract

a loose-based or springform cake tin, 20 cm diameter

serves 8–10

This luscious cheesecake is many people's favourite – there is something about the tartness of the fresh blueberries that contrasts so beautifully with the creamy cheese base.

Preheat the oven to 190°C (375°F) Gas 5.

Gently melt the butter in a saucepan, cool slightly and add the crushed biscuits. Press evenly into the base of the cake tin.

Beat the ingredients for the first layer together thoroughly, pour over the biscuit base and smooth the top. Place the tin on a baking tray and bake in the preheated oven for 20 minutes, or until just set. Set aside for 20 minutes to firm up.

Mix the ingredients for the second layer and spoon evenly over the first layer. Return to the oven for 10 minutes then remove from the oven and let cool. Refrigerate for at least 6 hours or overnight.

For the topping, heat the sugar gently with 2 tablespoons water until it dissolves. Turn up the heat, add the blueberries, cover and cook, shaking the pan occasionally for about 5 minutes until the berries are soft. Take off the heat. Mix the arrowroot with 2 tablespoons water and tip into the blueberries. Stir over a gentle heat until the juice has thickened. Set aside to cool then check for sweetness adding extra sugar to taste.

About an hour before serving ease a knife down the sides of the cake tin then release the clamp or push up the base. Spoon the blueberry topping evenly over the cheesecake and return to the fridge until ready to serve.

ricotta & muscatel raisin cheesecake

pastry

225 g fine polenta
75 g plain flour, plus extra for dusting
125 g caster sugar
55 g toasted pine nuts
175 g unsalted butter, cubed
2 large egg yolks

filling

75 g large Muscatel raisins
2–3 tablespoons Vin Santo or Marsala wine
500 g ricotta cheese
500 g full-fat soft cheese
240 ml sour cream
4 large eggs, separated
125 g caster sugar
2 teaspoons vanilla extract
a pinch of salt
freshly grated nutmeg

a springform cake tin, 23 cm diameter, greased and base-lined

serves 8–10

This classic baked cheesecake is delicious. For best results, make sure all the filling ingredients are at room temperature.

To make the pastry, put the polenta, flour, sugar, pine nuts and butter in a food processor and blend, in short bursts, until the mixture resembles coarse breadcrumbs. Add the egg yolks and process until the dough forms a ball. Wrap in clingfilm and chill for 1 hour.

Preheat the oven to 180°C (350°F) Gas 4. Roll out the pastry on a sheet of lightly floured, greaseproof paper to about 7 mm thickness and use to line the tin. Chill for 5 minutes. Cut out a large piece of baking parchment to fit the tin, put it on top of the pastry case, then fill with ceramic baking beans or rice. Bake in the preheated oven for 10 minutes. Remove the baking parchment and beans and return to the oven for a further 10 minutes. Let cool.

To make the filling, put the raisins in a bowl, add the Vin Santo and leave for several hours or overnight. (Alternatively, put the bowl in the microwave and heat on MEDIUM for 1 minute.) Put the ricotta cheese, soft cheese and sour cream in a large bowl and beat well. Put the egg yolks and sugar in a separate bowl and beat until light and creamy. Add the cheese mixture and vanilla extract and beat until smooth.

Put the egg whites and a pinch of salt in a separate, grease-free bowl. Whisk until soft peaks form, then fold into the cheese mixture. Spoon the filling into the pastry case and sprinkle nutmeg over the top. Bake in an oven preheated to 180°C (350°F) Gas 4 for 30–40 minutes, or until golden but still a little soft in the centre. Transfer to a wire rack and let cool. Serve at room temperature.

honey hazelnut crunch cheesecake

hazelnut praline
100 g whole unblanched hazelnuts
100 g caster sugar
Raspberry Sauce (page Strawberry Sauce variation page 233), to serve

filling
200 g caster sugar
55 g butter, softened
500 g full-fat soft cheese, at room temperature
25 g plain flour
2 tablespoons honey
5 eggs, separated
6 tablespoons single cream
1 teaspoon vanilla extract
½ teaspoon ground cinnamon
½ teaspoon ground nutmeg
55 g light soft brown sugar
75 g hazelnuts, toasted, skinned and coarsely chopped

a deep springform cake tin, 25 cm diameter, greased and floured

serves 10

This cheesecake is very easy to make and utterly delicious. Don't use a honey that is too strong or it will dominate the flavour – acacia or orange blossom is just fine.

To make the praline, first oil a large baking tray and set aside until needed. Put the hazelnuts and caster sugar in a saucepan and set over gentle heat until the sugar has melted. Do not stir. When melted, increase the heat and boil until the melted sugar turns to golden caramel. Immediately pour onto the prepared baking tray and let set and cool completely – about 1 hour. Break into pieces, then put in a blender or food processor and grind to a fine powder.

Preheat the oven to 160°C (325°F) Gas 3.

To make the filling, put the sugar and butter in a large bowl and beat until pale and fluffy. Add the soft cheese and beat until fluffy. Beat in the flour, honey and egg yolks. Stir in the cream, vanilla extract, spices and half the praline.

Put the egg whites in a separate, grease-free bowl and whisk until stiff peaks form. Gently fold into the cheese mixture, then pour into the prepared cake tin.

Put the soft brown sugar in a bowl and stir in the chopped hazelnuts, then sprinkle over the surface of the cheesecake. Bake in the preheated oven for 1 hour, then turn the oven off, leave the door ajar and let the cheesecake cool in the oven for about 2 hours. Alternatively, transfer the cheesecake to a wire rack and invert a large bowl over the cake so it cools slowly. Chill for 2 hours but serve at room temperature sprinkled with the remaining hazelnut praline and drizzled with Raspberry Sauce.

blackcurrant lake cheesecake

1 medium ready-made sponge flan case (at least 23 cm diameter)

filling
600 g tinned blackcurrants in fruit juice, drained and juice reserved
75 g caster sugar
60 ml crème de cassis
350 g full-fat soft cheese
2 eggs, separated
200 g double cream
7 g (1 sachet) powdered gelatine

topping
50 ml blackcurrant juice (if using fresh blackcurrants)
1 teaspoon powdered gelatine
fresh blackcurrants, dusted with icing sugar, to decorate

a springform cake tin, 23 cm diameter, oiled

serves 8

This deliciously light and tart mousse-style cheesecake gets its name from the shiny 'lake' of blackcurrant glaze on top.

Cut off the rim to level the flan case, then carefully slice the cake in half horizontally. Wrap and freeze one half for use another time. Using the base of the cake tin as a guide, put it on top of the sponge and cut round to make a 23 cm circle. Arrange the sponge in the bottom of the prepared tin.

Put the blackcurrants, sugar and crème de cassis in a blender and work to a smooth purée. Press through a sieve to remove the seeds. Set aside 2 tablespoons of the purée to make the glaze.

Put the soft cheese, egg yolks and cream in a bowl and beat well, then stir in the purée. Put the gelatine and 75 ml reserved juice in a small heatproof bowl and let stand for 5 minutes. Set the bowl over a saucepan of hot water and stir gently until the gelatine has dissolved, then stir into the cheese mixture. Put the egg whites in a grease-free bowl and whisk until stiff but not dry, then fold into the mixture. Pour into the tin and level the surface. Chill for 3–4 hours until firm.

To make the topping, put 50 ml reserved juice, the reserved purée and the 1 teaspoon powdered gelatine in a saucepan and mix well. Heat until the gelatine has dissolved, then cool until almost cold and just turning to syrup. Carefully pour over the surface of the cheesecake, making sure it covers the top. Chill for a further 1 hour. Carefully remove from the tin and set on a serving plate. Decorate with sugared blackcurrants and serve.

lemon & ginger cheesecake

225 g digestives or other wheaten biscuits
2 tablespoons caster sugar
2 teaspoons ground ginger
125 g unsalted butter, melted

filling
570 g cream cheese
180 g caster sugar
1 tablespoon cornflour
4 large eggs, beaten
grated zest of 2 unwaxed lemons
380 ml sour cream

topping
250 ml sour cream
2½ tablespoons caster sugar
80 g stem ginger in syrup, drained and finely chopped
finely grated zest of 1 unwaxed lemon

a springform cake tin, 25 cm diameter
a large roasting tin

serves 8–10

The water-bath method for cooking cheesecakes is quite simply the best way of producing a silky smooth, velvety-textured cheesecake that melts on the tongue.

Cover the outside of the cake tin with a double layer of foil, moulding it to the tin, but being careful not to puncture it so that it remains watertight. Line the base of the tin with baking parchment.

Preheat the oven to 180°C (350°F) Gas 4.

Put the biscuits in a food processor and pulse to form fine crumbs. Add the sugar and ground ginger and blend again. Transfer to a bowl and stir in the melted butter until evenly mixed. Spoon the crumbs into the prepared tin and press down to form an even layer on the base of the tin. Bake in the preheated oven for 10–12 minutes to set the crust, then let cool.

To make the filling, put the cream cheese and sugar in a large bowl and beat until smooth. Beat in the cornflour, followed by the eggs in about 4 batches. When smooth, beat in the lemon zest and sour cream. Pour the mixture over the crumb base. Set the cake tin in the roasting tin and pour very hot water into the roasting tin to come just over half-way up the sides of the cake tin. Transfer the tins to the oven and bake, at the same temperature, for 45–50 minutes or until the cheesecake is just set in the centre.

To make the topping, put the sour cream and 2 tablespoons of the sugar in a bowl and mix well. Remove the cheesecake from the oven and spread the sour cream mixture over the surface. Sprinkle the chopped ginger evenly over the top, then return to the oven for 10 minutes. Remove the cheesecake from its water bath, let cool on a wire rack, then chill, preferably overnight, before removing the foil and unmoulding the cheesecake. Toss the lemon zest with the remaining sugar sprinkle over the cheesecake just before serving.

meringues & soufflés

meringues with rosewater cream

3 egg whites
175 g caster sugar
¼ teaspoon ground cardamom
200 ml double cream
1 tablespoon clear honey
1 tablespoon rosewater
pomegranate seeds, to serve
(optional)

*a baking tray lined with
baking parchment*

serves 6

These light-as-air meringues are particularly good served with fresh pomegranate seeds, but work equally well with other fruits such as cherries, nectarines or peaches.

Preheat the oven to 160°C (325°F) Gas 3.

Put the egg whites in a grease-free bowl and whisk until they start to peak. Gradually whisk in the sugar, a spoonful at a time, until the mixture becomes very thick and glossy. Gently fold in the ground cardamom.

Drop 12 spoonfuls of the meringue mixture onto the prepared baking tray, leaving a gap between each mound. Bake in the preheated oven for 1 hour. Remove from the oven, transfer the meringues to a wire rack and let cool.

Put the cream, honey and rosewater into a bowl and whip until the mixture just holds its shape. Put a couple of spoonfuls of the whipped cream into each of six serving bowls, add two meringues to each one and top with the pomegranate seeds, if using.

raspberry & brown sugar meringues

4 large egg whites,
at room temperature
150 g unrefined caster sugar
50 g light brown muscovado sugar
200 g frozen raspberries,
not defrosted

*2 large baking trays, lined with
baking parchment*

makes 16 meringues

The little explosions of fruit in the middle of these meringues
are a real treat. They are best eaten within two to three hours
of making them.

Preheat the oven to 150°C (300°F) Gas 2.

Put the egg whites in a grease-free bowl and start to whisk them.
Increase the speed as they begin to froth up, moving the whisk
around the bowl, until they just hold a peak (about 2–3 minutes).
Gradually add the caster sugar a teaspoonful at a time, beating
the meringue well between each addition. When half the caster
sugar has been incorporated, add the rest of the caster sugar
a dessertspoonful at a time. Gradually add the brown sugar, then
gently fold in the frozen raspberries, ensuring that they are fully
coated by the meringue.

Using 2 dessertspoons, carefully spoon the meringues onto the
prepared baking trays. Place in the preheated oven and immediately
reduce the heat to 140°C (275°F) Gas 1. Bake for 1¼ hours until the
meringues are firm. Turn off the heat and leave the meringues to
cool in the oven.

You can refrigerate the meringues for up to 3 hours, lightly covered
with clingfilm, before serving.

passion fruit pavlovas

4 passion fruit

2 tablespoons freshly squeezed orange juice

2 teaspoons unrefined caster sugar, plus extra to taste

a few drops of orange flower water (optional)

4 bought meringue nests

4 heaped tablespoons lemon or orange curd

8 small scoops good-quality vanilla ice cream

serves 4

This is a simple-to-assemble, fresh-tasting and impressive dessert that uses ready-made meringue nests. Perfect for mid-week entertaining when time is short.

Halve the passion fruit and scoop the pulp and seeds into a small bowl, taking care not to include any of the bitter pith.

Add the orange juice and sugar to the bowl and stir well to combine. Check for sweetness, adding a little orange flower water and/or extra sugar to taste.

Put a meringue nest on each of four serving plates and spoon the curd into the base. Top with two balls of vanilla ice cream and spoon over the orange and passion fruit sauce. Serve immediately.

chocolate &
strawberry pavlova

1 recipe Bitter Chocolate Sauce
or Rich Chocolate Fudge Sauce
(page 229), warmed

4 large egg whites

a pinch of salt

225 g unrefined caster sugar,
plus extra to taste

1 teaspoon cornflour

1 tablespoon cocoa powder

1 teaspoon vanilla extract

1 teaspoon white wine vinegar

125 g dark chocolate
(60–70% cocoa solids), grated

450 ml double cream

450 g fresh strawberries, hulled

*a baking tray, lined with non-stick
baking parchment on which a circle,
23 cm diameter, has been drawn*

serves 6

Strawberries and chocolate are one of those great flavour combinations. You can keep the cooled meringue in an airtight container until ready to use so it's possible to start preparing this dessert a day or two ahead.

Preheat the oven to 140°C (275°F) Gas 1.

Whisk the egg whites with the salt in a large, grease-free bowl until very stiff. Gradually whisk in the caster sugar, 1 tablespoon at a time, making sure the meringue is 'bouncily' stiff between each addition of sugar. Whisk the cornflour, cocoa, vanilla extract and vinegar into the egg whites, then fold in the grated chocolate.

Spoon the meringue onto the marked circle right to the edges – the meringue will spread to approximately 30 cm as it cooks. Bake for about 45 minutes until it is beginning to turn pale brown and has collapsed a little. Remove from the oven and let cool.

Whip the cream to soft peaks with a little sugar to taste. Carefully peel the paper from the meringue. Cut it into six wedges and arrange them on a large serving plate, slightly overlapping the slices. Generously top with the whipped cream and spread out with a spatula. Pile the strawberries on top and serve immediately, drizzled with the your choice of warm chocolate sauce.

almond meringue & chocolate layer cake

almond meringue rounds
6 large egg whites
180 g caster sugar
180 g ground almonds
2 tablespoons cornflour

chocolate ganache
400 ml double cream
300 g dark chocolate, finely chopped, plus extra to grate on top

topping
300 ml whipping cream
2 tablespoons caster sugar

3 baking trays, lined with non-stick baking parchment on which circles, 20 cm diameter, have been drawn

a piping bag, fitted with a wide nozzle (optional)

serves 6–8

This layered meringue cake is filled with a chocolate ganache and topped with whipped cream. It's very simple to prepare but makes an impressive dessert for a special occasion.

Preheat the oven to 120°C (250°F) Gas ½. Mark the centre point of the 3 parchment paper circles and put the paper on the trays. Set aside until needed.

To make the meringues, put the egg whites and 2 tablespoons sugar in a bowl and beat until firm peaks form. Put the remaining sugar, the ground almonds and cornflour in another bowl and mix well. Gently fold the dry ingredients into the beaten whites until blended.

Transfer one-third of the meringue into the pastry bag. Starting at the middle of a circle, pipe out a round in a spiral, until you reach the marked edge. Repeat to make 2 more rounds. Alternatively, spread the meringue inside the circles with a small spatula, taking care to spread in an even layer so it cooks evenly. Bake in the preheated oven for 1½–2 hours until firm and dry. Let cool.

To make the ganache, put the cream in a saucepan and bring just to the boil. Remove from the heat and stir in the chocolate until completely melted. Let cool slightly.

To assemble, put 1 meringue on an attractive serving plate. Top with one-third of the ganache. Put another meringue on top, add another third of the ganache, then top with the remaining meringue and the remaining chocolate ganache. Chill in the fridge until the chocolate has completely cooled.

Whip the cream and sugar until firm and spread on top of the final chocolate layer. Grate some chocolate over the top and chill until ready to serve, at least 3 hours or up to 24 hours. Serve chilled.

floating islands

6 egg whites
3 tablespoons icing sugar
flaked almonds, to serve

custard sauce
500 ml full-fat milk
(or half milk, half single cream)
1 vanilla pod, split lengthways
5 large egg yolks
75 g caster sugar

caramel
100 g caster sugar
freshly squeezed lemon juice

6 small microwave-proof ramekins

serves 6

This is a simple microwave version of the classic French dessert, also called Oeufs à la Neige. The sauce and egg whites can be made a few hours in advance, but the caramel must be last-minute.

To make the custard sauce, put the milk and vanilla pod in a saucepan and bring just to the boil. Remove from the heat, cover and leave to infuse for 15 minutes.

Put the egg yolks and sugar in a heatproof bowl and whisk until slightly thickened and pale yellow. Gradually stir the hot milk into the egg yolk mixture, then return all to the saucepan set over very low heat. Continue stirring until the mixture is thick enough to coat the back of the spoon, about 2–3 minutes. Do not let it boil or it will curdle. Remove from the heat and let cool.

Put the egg whites and icing sugar in a bowl and beat until stiff. Divide the whites between six ramekins, filling to the top. Put two ramekins in the middle of the microwave, making sure the dishes touch in the middle of the oven. Cook on LOW for 30 seconds. Check, and then repeat for 30 seconds more. The eggs will puff up like a soufflé. If they are not completely firm through, cook for a further 30 seconds. Repeat until all six ramekins are cooked. Prise the 'islands' gently out of the ramekins.

When ready to serve, put 2–3 spoonfuls of custard sauce in each of six shallow soup plates. Put an egg-white puff in the middle of each, then prepare the caramel.

Put the caster sugar, a squeeze of lemon juice and 3 tablespoons water in a heavy saucepan and cook, stirring, until it turns a light caramel colour. Trickle some caramel over each egg white puff and sprinkle with the almonds. Serve at room temperature.

baked alaska

500 ml strawberry
or vanilla ice cream
4 egg whites
230 g caster sugar
150 g fresh raspberries
icing sugar, for dusting

sponge base
115 g plain flour
1 teaspoon baking powder
115 g caster sugar
115 g unsalted butter, softened
½ teaspoon vanilla extract
2 large eggs, beaten
1 tablespoon milk

*a sandwich cake tin or
springform cake tin, 21 cm diameter,
greased and base-lined*

serves 6

This classic dessert looks very impressive but is simple to make. To speed things up even more, you can use a ready-made sponge flan case or cake for the base.

Preheat the oven to 180°C (350°F) Gas 4.

To make the sponge base, sift the flour and baking powder into a mixing bowl and stir in the sugar. Add the butter and vanilla extract. Beat the eggs and the milk together and beat until the mixture is very smooth and light. Spoon the cake mixture into the prepared tin and level the surface.

Bake in the preheated oven for about 25 minutes, until light golden brown and the centre of the cake springs back with lightly pressed. Remove from the oven, let cool for 2 minutes, then carefully turn out onto a wire rack and let cool completely.

Remove the ice cream from the freezer and leave until soft enough to spoon onto the sponge; put the sponge cake onto a baking tray, then scoop or spoon the ice cream on top to make an even layer. Put the whole thing back into the freezer and leave until very firm – at least 1 hour, but you can leave it in the freezer for up to 3 days.

When you are ready to serve, preheat the oven to 220°C (425°F) Gas 7. Put the egg whites in a grease-free bowl and whisk until frothy. Add the caster sugar and whisk until stiff and glossy.

Remove the sponge and ice cream from the freezer. Arrange the raspberries on top of the ice cream. Quickly cover the whole thing with the meringue, spreading it evenly and making sure that there are no holes or gaps. Dust with sifted icing sugar. Bake in the preheated oven for just 4–5 minutes, until lightly browned. Serve immediately.

lemon meringue pie

1 recipe Sweet Tart Pastry (page 42)

lemon filling

1 large whole egg and 3 large
eggs yolks

125 g caster sugar

finely grated zest and
freshly squeezed juice of
2 large lemons

125 g unsalted butter,
melted and cooled

125 ml whipping cream

meringue

3 large egg whites

¼ teaspoon cream of tartar

125 g caster sugar,
plus 1 tablespoon

½ teaspoon finely grated
lemon zest

*a loose-based
tart tin, 20–23 cm diameter*

serves 6–8

A cloud of fluffy, crisp-crusted meringue tops a creamy,
lemon curd filling to create a texture and taste sensation.

Roll out the pastry and use to line the tart tin. Bake blind following
the method given on page 42.

Preheat the oven to 170°C (325°F) Gas 3.

For the lemon filling, put the egg, egg yolks and sugar in a bowl and
beat until slightly thickened and a pale yellow. Beat in the lemon
zest, butter, cream and finally the lemon juice. Pour the filling into
the pastry case and bake in the preheated oven for 20–30 minutes
until the filling is barely set in the centre. Do not let it overbake.

To make the meringue, put the egg whites and cream of tartar in
a grease-free bowl and whisk until frothy. Whisk in half the sugar
until the meringue is stiff and glossy. Fold in the remaining sugar
and the lemon zest using a metal spoon. Pile the meringue onto the
tart, swirling and peaking as you go. Sprinkle with the 1 tablespoon
sugar and return the tart to the oven for another 30–35 minutes or
until the meringue is browned and crisp on the outside. Serve warm
or cold.

variation If time is short you can make a very easy lemon meringue
pie by filling the pastry case with homemade or good-quality bought
lemon curd, then topping with the meringue and baking as above.

fresh fig & walnut meringue

150 g walnut halves
8–10 small fresh figs, halved
6 large egg whites
230 g soft light brown sugar

a baking tray, lined with non-stick baking parchment on which a circle, 23 cm in diameter, has been drawn

serves 8–10

Don't use big figs here, as they will split and prevent the egg whites from cooking and the meringue will become sloppy.

Preheat the oven to 180°C (350°F) Gas 4.

Put the walnuts on a baking tray and toast in the preheated oven for 5 minutes, until just starting to turn golden. Remove and let cool. Leave the oven on.

Put the egg whites in a large, grease-free bowl and beat until frothy. Add a tablespoon of the sugar at a time, beating well between each addition, and continue until all the sugar has been added and the meringue resembles a thick, fluffy caramel. Add the figs and walnuts and stir to combine.

Spoon the mixture onto the paper on the baking tray, keeping within the circle and using the back of a large spoon to create dents and peaks. Bake in the preheated oven for 40–45 minutes, until the peaks of the meringue are a dark golden colour.

Let cool for 15 minutes then slide a large pallette knife or metal fish slice under the meringue to remove it from the paper and transfer it to a serving plate. Best eaten warm or at room temperature.

strawberry meringue roulade

170 g caster sugar,
plus 2 teaspoons

3 egg whites

1 teaspoon cornflour

125 ml whipping cream

3 tablespoons icing sugar,
plus extra for dusting

250 g fresh strawberries,
hulled and sliced

*a baking tray, lined with
baking parchment*

serves 4–6

It doesn't matter if this meringue splits or isn't crispy; it's not meant to be. It's really just an excuse to eat lots of fresh strawberries and cream!

Preheat the oven to 130°C (250°F) Gas ½.

Sprinkle with the baking parchment on the baking tray with 1 teaspoon of the caster sugar.

Put the egg whites in a grease-free bowl, add the cornflour and whisk until soft peaks form. Add 1 tablespoon of sugar at a time, beating well between each addition, and continue beating until you can no longer feel grains of sugar when you rub the mixture between your thumb and forefinger.

Spoon the mixture onto the prepared baking tray and smooth it out with a palette knife to a rectangle about 20 x 30 cm and no thicker than 1 cm. Bake the meringue in the preheated oven for 20 minutes, until it is just set and the top is a light caramel colour.

Take a second piece of baking parchment, slightly larger than the meringue, and sprinkle over 1 teaspoon caster sugar. Quickly flip the tray upside-down so that the meringue is turned out onto the paper. Peel off the bottom piece of baking parchment. Firmly roll the meringue up into a log with the second sheet of paper and wrap in a clean tea towel. Let cool completely.

Put the cream and icing sugar in a bowl and whisk until firm peaks form. Unroll the meringue. Spoon the cream over the meringue, leaving a 2-cm margin around the edge. Arrange the sliced strawberries over the cream and roll up. Dust liberally with icing sugar just before serving.

hot chocolate soufflé

1 tablespoon softened butter

3 tablespoons caster sugar, plus extra for sprinkling

180 g dark chocolate, chopped

150 ml double cream

3 large eggs, separated

2 tablespoons Cognac or brandy

2 large egg whites

icing sugar, for dusting

4 soufflé dishes, 300 ml capacity, or 4 large ceramic cups, buttered and sugared (see recipe method)

serves 4

These delicious soufflés, with their light and meltingly soft texture, are more like a hot chocolate mousse than a soufflé. Serve with little crisp biscuits, such as Langue du Chat.

Brush the soufflé dishes with a little melted butter, then sprinkle with sugar to give an even coating. Stand the dishes on a baking tray or in a shallow roasting tin.

Put the chocolate into a medium, heavy-based saucepan, pour in the cream, then set over very low heat and stir frequently until melted and smooth. Remove from the heat and stir in the egg yolks, one at a time, followed by the Cognac. At this point the mixture can be covered and set aside for up to 2 hours.

Preheat the oven to 220°C (425°F) Gas 7.

Put the 5 egg whites into a grease-free bowl and whisk until soft peaks form. Gradually whisk in the 3 tablespoons caster sugar to give a glossy, stiff meringue. The chocolate mixture should feel comfortably warm to your finger, so gently reheat if necessary. Using a large metal spoon, add a little of the meringue to the chocolate mixture and mix thoroughly. This loosens the consistency, making it easier to incorporate the rest of the meringue. Pour the chocolate mixture on top of the remaining meringue and gently fold them together until just blended.

Spoon the mixture into the soufflé dishes – the mixture should come to just below the rim. Bake in the preheated oven for 8–10 minutes, until barely set – the centres should be soft and wobble when gently shaken. Dust with icing sugar and serve immediately.

black forest soufflé with hot chocolate sauce

1 recipe Bitter Chocolate Sauce or White Chocolate Sauce (page 229), to serve

300 g dark chocolate, broken into small pieces (60–70% cocoa solids)

100 g drained amarena cherries

4 egg yolks

250 ml egg whites*

100 g unrefined caster sugar

6 large ramekins, buttered and dusted with caster sugar

serves 6

* Egg whites are given as a liquid measurement in this recipe to ensure a good result – you will need 3–6 whites depending on the size of eggs used.

Italian amarena cherries are addictive. Reserve the drained syrup and stir it into the bitter chocolate sauce, if using.

Preheat the oven to 220°C (425°F) Gas 7.

Put the chocolate in a heatproof bowl and set it over a saucepan of simmering, not boiling, water. The base of the bowl must not touch the water. Stir the chocolate gently until it has completely melted. Remove from the heat and set aside.

Divide the amarena cherries between the ramekins.

Beat the egg yolks into the melted chocolate with a wooden spoon until the mixture becomes thick and stiff.

Whisk the egg whites in a grease-free bowl until they form soft peaks. Add the sugar and continue to whisk until the whites form soft peaks again and are thick and smooth. Whisk a large tablespoon of the meringue into the chocolate mixture, then carefully fold in the remaining meringue with a metal spoon.

Divide the mixture between the ramekins and give each one a good tap on the work surface to level the top. Set them on a heavy baking tray or shallow roasting tin.

Bake in the preheated oven for 13–15 minutes, or until they are well risen. Serve immediately with your choice of chocolate sauce.

vanilla orange soufflé

250 ml full cream milk

1 vanilla pod, split lengthways

1 tablespoon freshly grated orange zest

4 large egg yolks

6 egg whites

100 g caster sugar

3 tablespoons plain flour

1 tablespoon Grand Marnier or other orange-flavoured liqueur (optional)

a soufflé dish, about 16 cm diameter, buttered and dusted with icing sugar

serves 4

A lot of fuss is made about making soufflés, but it's really not that complicated. The main mixture can be prepared ahead of time, leaving you with nothing more than whisking egg whites and baking just before serving.

Put the milk and vanilla pod in a saucepan set over medium heat. Bring just to the boil, then cover and set aside for 15 minutes.

Put the orange zest, egg yolks and all but 1 tablespoon of the sugar in a large bowl and whisk until slightly thickened and a pale yellow colour. Whisk in the flour and the Grand Marnier, if using.

Scrape the vanilla seeds into the milk, then discard the pod. Gradually whisk the hot milk into the yolk mixture, then return to the saucepan and set over low heat. Cook, stirring constantly with a wooden spoon, until thick enough to coat the back of the spoon, about 2–3 minutes. Let cool. (The recipe can be made up to 24 hours in advance to this stage, then cover and chill until needed.)

Preheat the oven to 200°C (400°F) Gas 6.

Put the egg whites and remaining sugar in a separate grease-free bowl and beat until firm and glossy. Fold one-third of the egg whites into the cooled orange mixture until blended, then carefully but thoroughly fold in the rest.

Transfer to the prepared soufflé dish and put in the oven. Lower the heat to 180°C (350°F) Gas 4. Bake until puffed and just browned, about 20–30 minutes. Serve immediately.

mousses, jellies & trifles

classic chocolate mousse

85 g dark chocolate, finely chopped

2 tablespoons brandy, rum or water

10 g unsalted butter, at room temperature

3 large eggs, separated

4 individual serving dishes, cups or glasses

serves 4

This French classic relies on just three ingredients – the finest chocolate, the freshest eggs and unsalted butter – so do buy the best you can find.

Put the chocolate and brandy into a heatproof bowl set over a saucepan of simmering but not boiling water and leave until just melted (do not let the base of the bowl touch the water). Remove the bowl from the heat and gently stir in the butter (it is vital to melt the chocolate gently without letting it get too hot, and to stir as little as possible). Leave for 1 minute, then gently stir in the egg yolks, one at a time.

Put the egg whites into a grease-free bowl and whisk until stiff peaks form. Stir about one-quarter of the egg whites into the chocolate mixture to loosen it then, using a large metal spoon, gently fold in the rest of the egg whites in 3 batches. Carefully spoon into serving bowls, then chill for 2 hours before serving.

variations

espresso mousse Make the recipe above, replacing the brandy with 3 tablespoons of good-quality espresso coffee, and whisking 3 tablespoons caster sugar into the stiff egg whites before adding them to the chocolate mixture.

cappuccino mousse This is a creamy version of the espresso mousse above. Put 125 ml whipping cream into a mixing bowl and whisk until soft peaks form. Fold half the cream into the mousse after the egg whites, then spoon into small coffee cups and chill for 2 hours. Just before serving, spoon the rest of the cream on top of the mousse, then sprinkle with cocoa.

mint chocolate mousse

150 g dark chocolate
(60–70% cocoa solids)

4–6 dark chocolate-covered mint
fondants (preferably After Eights),
chopped

4 eggs, separated

2 tablespoons unrefined caster sugar

4 tablespoons double cream

1 teaspoon powdered gelatine

2 tablespoons chopped chocolate
mint sticks, to decorate

4 individual serving dishes or glasses

serves 4

For all those who love mint and dark chocolate, this is for you, especially if you're a fan of after-dinner mints covered in dark chocolate. The mousse is relatively simple to make and is a good dinner-party standby.

Put the chocolate and chocolate-covered mints into a heatproof bowl set over a saucepan of simmering but not boiling water and leave until just melted (do not let the base of the bowl touch the water). Leave to cool slightly.

Whisk together the egg yolks and sugar in a large bowl until thick and mousse-like, then whisk in the melted chocolate mixture and the cream.

Sprinkle the gelatine over 4 tablespoons water in a small, heatproof bowl and leave to soak and swell for 2–3 minutes. Put the bowl into a pan of simmering water and stir until the gelatine has dissolved. Whisk into the chocolate mixture.

Working quickly, whisk the egg whites in a grease-free bowl until stiff, then fold into the chocolate mixture with a metal spoon.

Divide the mousse between the pots. Scatter with the chopped mint sticks, then chill until set. Leave at cool room temperature for about 20 minutes before serving.

chocolate orange mousse

1 teaspoon finely grated orange zest

2 tablespoons Grand Marnier or other orange-flavoured liqueur

250 g dark chocolate (60%–70% cocoa solids), roughly chopped

4 eggs, separated

250 ml single or whipping cream

chopped unsalted pistachios, to decorate

6 individual serving dishes or glasses

serves 6

This is an adults-only version of a classic chocolate mousse – it's very rich and slightly tipsy.

Put the orange zest, Grand Marnier and chocolate in a heatproof bowl set over a saucepan of simmering but not boiling water (do not let the base of the bowl touch the water). Stir occasionally until the chocolate has melted and the mixture is smooth and glossy. Remove from the heat and let cool for 5 minutes.

Whisk the egg yolks, one at a time, into the chocolate mixture until smooth. Beat the egg whites in a grease-free bowl until softly peaking, being careful not to overbeat them. Fold them into the chocolate mixture in two batches. Whisk the cream to soft peaks then gently fold it into the chocolate and egg mixture until well combined.

Spoon into 6 small serving dishes. Cover and chill for a minimum of 3 hours. Sprinkle with chopped pistachios just before serving.

mango mousse with tropical fruit salad

350 g ripe mango flesh
1–2 tablespoons caster sugar
finely grated zest and juice
of 2 unwaxed limes
7 g powdered gelatine (1 sachet)
150 ml double cream, lightly whipped
2 egg whites

lemongrass syrup
125 g sugar
½ stick lemongrass,
bruised with a rolling pin
finely grated zest and juice
of 1 unwaxed lime

tropical fruit salad
a selection of fresh exotic fruit,
such as papaya, pineapple,
yellow melon, lychees and grapes
(you will need about 75 g
prepared fruit per person)
seeds from 1 very ripe pomegranate

*4 individual serving dishes
or glasses*

serves 4

Brightly coloured fruits are tossed in a fragrant lemongrass and lime syrup, then piled on top of a light yet rich mango mousse – a refreshing end to a summer meal.

Put the mangoes in a blender or food processor, add sugar to taste and the lime zest and juice and blend to make a smooth, soft purée.

Put 3 tablespoons water in a saucepan, sprinkle with the gelatine and leave for 5 minutes to swell and sponge. Set the saucepan over low heat until the gelatine has dissolved and the liquid is clear. Add the mango purée and stir well.

Remove from the heat, transfer the mixture to a bowl and chill for 15 minutes to set slightly then fold in the cream. Whisk the egg whites until softly peaking and carefully fold into the mango mixture. Spoon into individual glasses, leaving enough room to top with fruit salad. Chill for 2–3 hours until set.

To make the lemongrass syrup, put the sugar in a small heavy-based saucepan, add 300 ml water and melt over low heat. When the sugar has completely dissolved, add the lemongrass, increase the heat and boil for about 2–3 minutes until the syrup feels slippery when tested between the fingers. Remove from the heat, remove the lemongrass and add the lime juice. Let cool, then stir in the lime zest. Chill until ready to use.

Peel and deseed the fruit and cut it into slices or chunks. Put it in a bowl and stir to combine. Add the chilled syrup and mix again to coat, then chill in the fridge.

To serve, spoon the fruit salad on top of the set mousses and sprinkle with the pomegranate seeds.

raspberry cream

350 g raspberries,
fresh or frozen and defrosted

5–6 tablespoons
caster sugar, to taste

250 ml whipping cream, chilled

1 large egg white

1 small punnet of fresh raspberries

sprigs of fresh mint, to serve

4 individual serving dishes or glasses

serves 4

This deliciously light and airy mousse can also be made with strawberries or mixed berries, though you will have to adjust the sugar content.

Put the raspberries in a blender or food processor and blend until smooth, then press through a sieve to obtain a smooth purée; you should have about 200 ml. Stir in 4–5 tablespoons of the sugar. Set aside.

Put the cream in a large bowl and whisk until it holds firm peaks. Set aside.

Beat the egg white with the remaining tablespoon of the sugar until it holds firm peaks. Fold the beaten egg white and raspberry purée into the cream.

Divide the mixture between 4 serving glasses, filling half-way. Set aside 4 fresh raspberries, then divide the remaining fresh ones between the glasses and top with the remaining raspberry cream.

Decorate the top of each with a fresh raspberry and a mint sprig. Chill for up to 6 hours. Serve cold.

variation If preferred, you can use fromage frais in place of the whipped cream, or use half whipped cream and half fromage frais.

blueberry fool

500 g fresh blueberries,
washed and picked over
100–125 g caster sugar, to taste

custard
250 ml milk
1 vanilla pod
2 egg yolks
1 tablespoon caster sugar
2 teaspoons cornflour

*4–6 individual serving dishes
or glasses*

serves 4–6

Fruit fools are the epitome of English country summer food. To save time, use single cream instead of custard – simply mix it into the cooked fruit before pouring into the glasses.

To make the custard, put the milk in a small saucepan with the vanilla pod and bring slowly to simmering point. Remove the vanilla pod, rinse, dry and put to one side.

Whisk the egg yolks in a bowl with the sugar and cornflour and slowly add the warmed milk, whisking as you do so. Strain the mixture back into the saucepan and stir continuously over low heat with a wire whisk until the mixture thickens. Pour into a clean shallow bowl to cool.

Put the blueberries in a saucepan. Add the sugar, to taste, cover and cook over low heat for 3–4 minutes or until just tender. Transfer to a food processor and reduce to a smooth purée. When cool, transfer to a bowl and stir in the custard. Spoon into serving glasses and chill until ready to serve.

strawberry, rose & rhubarb fool

400 g fresh rhubarb

3 tablespoons unrefined caster sugar

225 g fresh, ripe strawberries, plus extra to decorate

2–3 tablespoons rose syrup or rosewater and extra caster sugar

300 g Greek-style yoghurt

285 ml whipping cream

6 individual serving dishes or glasses

serves 6

Rhubarb and strawberries have an extraordinary taste affinity and luckily come into season at the same time of year.

Slice the rhubarb and put it in a saucepan with the sugar and 2 tablespoons water. Put a lid on the pan and set over low heat until the fruit comes to the boil, then turn the heat down and simmer for 7–10 minutes until the fruit is soft. Tip the fruit into a sieve over a bowl and drain off the juice.

Hull the strawberries, put 225 g of them in a food processor and whizz until smooth. Add the drained rhubarb and 1 tablespoon rose syrup or 2 teaspoons rosewater with 1 tablespoon caster sugar and whizz again. Tip the purée into a bowl and leave to cool. Tip the yoghurt into a large bowl. In a separate bowl, whip the cream until just holding its shape and sweeten to taste with rose syrup or rosewater and sugar. Fold half the cream into the yoghurt. Fold half the puréed strawberry and rhubarb into the yoghurt and cream mixture then lightly mix the remaining cream and the rest of the rhubarb and strawberry purée to create a marbled effect.

Spoon the fool into individual glasses and chill until ready to serve. Slice the remaining strawberries and sprinkle with a few drops of rose syrup or a little sugar. Use the strawberry slices to decorate the top of each glass.

orange & cointreau syllabub

150 ml French Muscat or other strong sweet white wine (minimum 15% ABV)

1 tablespoon Cointreau or other orange-flavoured liqueur

finely grated zest of 2 oranges

2 tablespoons freshly squeezed orange juice

2 tablespoons freshly squeezed lemon juice

4 tablespoons unrefined caster sugar

400 ml double cream, chilled

a large bowl, chilled for 30–40 minutes in the fridge or for 15–20 minutes in the freezer

6 small glass tumblers or serving dishes

serves 6

Syllabub is a delicious, velvety smooth concoction of sweet wine and cream. This one is topped with an irresistibly crunchy mixture of orange zest and sugar.

Pour the wine into a bowl, add the Cointreau, half the orange zest, the orange and lemon juices and 2 tablespoons of the sugar. Stir, cover and refrigerate for several hours or overnight then strain the mixture through a fine sieve.

Pour the cream into the chilled bowl and whisk until it starts to thicken. Gradually add the orange-flavoured wine, beating between each addition until the cream thickens again. (Don't overbeat it, or it will separate.) Aim for a thick pouring consistency. When the final addition of wine has been incorporated, the mixture should hold a trail when you lift out the beaters, but shouldn't be stiff. Ladle the mixture into tumblers and chill for at least an hour before serving.

Mix the remaining orange zest and sugar, and leave it on a plate to crisp up. Sprinkle the orange sugar over the top of each glass to serve.

vin santo trifle

250 g Italian biscotti
100 ml vin santo
8 ripe figs, quartered lengthways
one 425-g tin amarena cherries in syrup, drained
500 ml double cream
500 g mascarpone cheese
75 g unrefined caster sugar
50 g flaked almonds
50 g white chocolate

a large serving bowl, preferably glass

serves 8

Instead of the traditional egg custard, this quick and easy trifle uses a mixture of cream and mascarpone cheese. Go to an Italian deli for vin santo (a delicious sweet wine) and biscotti (hard, almond-flavoured Italian biscuits).

Arrange the biscotti in the bottom of the serving bowl.

Pour over the vin santo, making sure that all of the biscotti are moistened. Arrange the figs and cherries on top.

Put the cream in a bowl and whip lightly until soft peaks form. Add the mascarpone and sugar and continue whisking until the mixture is stiff.

Spoon the cream and mascarpone mixture over the fruit, then sprinkle with almonds. Using a vegetable peeler, make curls with the white chocolate and sprinkle over the trifle. Chill until ready to serve.

tiramisù

50 amaretti biscuits, crushed

200 ml Kahlúa or other coffee-flavoured liqueur

6 tablespoons brandy

100 ml strong black coffee

1 kg mascarpone cheese, at room temperature

12 eggs, separated

100 g caster sugar

250 g dark chocolate, grated, or 4 tablespoons cocoa powder

20 glasses or large square or rectangular serving dish

serves 20

Foolproof and very quick to prepare, tiramisù is a wonderful dessert to serve a large group of people – it can be made in advance, doesn't need cooking and tastes quite delicious.

Arrange a quarter of the crushed amaretti biscuits at the bottom of the glasses or serving dish. Put the Kahlúa in a small bowl with the brandy and coffee and mix to combine. Pour a quarter of the mixture over the crushed biscuits.

Put the mascarpone, egg yolks and caster sugar in a bowl and beat until smooth and lump-free. Put the egg whites in a separate, grease-free bowl and whisk until stiff and peaking. Gently fold the egg whites into the mascarpone mixture.

Spoon a quarter of the mixture over the biscuits, then repeat the layers 3 times, finishing with a layer of mascarpone mixture.

Sprinkle the chocolate or cocoa over the top of the tiramisù and chill overnight. Serve chilled or at room temperature.

poached pear tiramisù

6–8 sponge fingers (savoiardi)
250 ml Marsala or brandy
115 g caster sugar
2 pears, peeled, cored and cut into eighths
2 egg whites
4 egg yolks
250 g mascarpone cheese, at room temperature
1 tablespoon cocoa powder

4 individual serving dishes or glasses

serves 4

This has all the elements of a perfect dessert – alcohol, creamy custard and cocoa. Do choose your pears carefully. Soft and sweet varieties do not poach well and can turn into an overly sweet mush – choose a firm brown variety instead.

Line the bottom of each serving dish with the sponge fingers, breaking them into pieces as necessary.

Put the Marsala, half the sugar and 125 ml water in a non-stick frying pan and cook over high heat until the mixture boils, stirring until the sugar has dissolved. Add the pears and cook at a gentle simmer for 20 minutes, turning the pears often, until they are soft and glossy and the liquid has reduced by half. Lay the pears on top of the biscuits and spoon or pour over the poaching liquid.

Whisk the egg whites in a grease-free bowl until firmly peaking. Beat the 4 egg yolks with the remaining sugar for 4–5 minutes, or until pale yellow and doubled in size. Beat in the mascarpone until the mixture is creamy and lump-free.

Using a large spoon, gently fold the egg whites into the egg and mascarpone mixture and spoon it over the pears. Chill for at least 3 hours. Dust with cocoa just before serving.

strawberry tiramisù

400 g fresh strawberries
5 amaretti biscuits
2 large eggs, separated
40 g unrefined caster sugar
¼ teaspoon vanilla extract
4 tablespoons white rum
250 g mascarpone cheese,
at room temperature
3 tablespoons whipping cream
100 ml pressed apple juice
100 g sponge fingers (savoiardi)

a large serving bowl, preferably glass

serves 6

This is an adaptation of the classic tiramisù recipe. The combination of almond-flavoured amaretti biscuits and fresh strawberries works surprisingly well.

Hull the strawberries. Weigh out 100 g and chop them finely. Slice the remaining strawberries and set aside. Put the amaretti biscuits in a plastic bag, seal, then hit them with a rolling pin until they are the consistency of coarse breadcrumbs.

Whisk the egg yolks until pale yellow and fluffy, gradually adding the sugar as you go. Add the vanilla extract and a tablespoon of the rum. Put the mascarpone cheese in a large bowl, beat with a wooden spoon to soften, then gradually add the egg yolk mixture and beat until smooth and lump-free. In a separate grease-free bowl, whisk the egg whites until they are softly peaking. Fold the chopped strawberries into the mascarpone cheese mixture, then carefully fold in the egg whites.

Whip the whipping cream to a similar consistency then fold that in too, together with a third of the crushed amaretti biscuits. Mix the remaining rum with the apple juice. Dip some of the savoiardi in the apple-rum mixture and lay across the base of the serving bowl. Reserving some sliced strawberries for decoration, arrange a layer of strawberries over the biscuits, then cover with a layer of mascarpone cream. Repeat with 1 or 2 more layers of soaked biscuits (reserving some to decorate), strawberries and mascarpone cream, finishing with the mascarpone cream. Chill for at least 5 hours before serving.

About 1 hour before you serve, sprinkle the remaining amaretti crumbs over the top of the tiramisù and decorate with the sliced strawberries. Return the tiramisù to the fridge until ready to serve.

crème caramel

750 ml full-fat milk
1 vanilla pod, split lengthways
180 g sugar
2 pinches of salt
5 large eggs

8 ramekins
a large roasting tin

serves 8

Crème caramel is simple to make, but there are a few tricks to help you with unmoulding. Don't use ramekins that are too deep and don't overfill them. Leave the ramekins in the bain-marie for at least 15 minutes before removing them.

Preheat the oven to 180°C (350°F) Gas 4.

Put the milk, vanilla pod and its seeds in a saucepan over medium heat and bring just to the boil. Immediately remove from the heat, cover and let stand while you make the caramel.

To make the caramel, put 100 g of the sugar; a pinch of salt and 4 tablespoons water in a small, heavy-based saucepan, preferably with a pouring lip. Heat until the sugar turns a deep caramel colour, then remove from the heat. When it stops sizzling, pour carefully into the ramekins. Take care not to let the caramel come into contact with your skin; it will be very hot. Set the ramekins in the roasting tin and add enough boiling water to the tin to come half-way up the sides of the ramekins – this is called a bain-marie. Set aside.

Add the remaining 80 g sugar and another pinch of salt to the saucepan of warm milk and stir until dissolved. Remove the vanilla pod. Put the eggs in a separate bowl and whisk until smooth. Pour the warm milk into the eggs and stir well. Ladle into the ramekins.

Carefully transfer the roasting tin with the filled ramekins to the preheated oven and bake until the custard has set and a knife inserted into the middle comes out clean, about 20–25 minutes. Serve at room temperature either in their ramekins or inverted onto a plate so the caramel forms a pool of sweet sauce.

crema catalana

200 g caster sugar
4 teaspoons cornflour
6 large egg yolks
600 ml double cream
400 ml full-fat milk
freshly grated zest from
1 unwaxed lemon
½ cinnamon stick

6 shallow ovenproof dishes,
10.5 cm diameter x 2.5 cm deep
a cook's blowtorch

serves 6

This classic Spanish dish is similar to the French crème brûlée. It is served in small cazuelas (see note) filled right to the top so that the surface can be caramelized with a branding iron that has been heated over flame. You'll need to use a blowtorch – household grills aren't hot enough.

Mix 150 g of the sugar and the cornflour in a bowl. Stir in the egg yolks until smooth, but do not whisk or the mixture will form a froth.

Put the cream, milk, lemon zest and cinnamon in a saucepan and heat gently until it just reaches boiling point. Pour onto the egg yolk mixture and stir well. Rinse out the pan and add the mixture. Stir over a low heat with a wooden spoon until it thickens enough to coat the spoon. Remove from the heat, leave to infuse for about 30 minutes, then strain into a jug. Pour into the 6 serving dishes and chill for about 12 hours.

Sprinkle over the remaining sugar and caramelize the sugar with a blowtorch. As the caramel cools, it will harden. The dishes can be left for up to 1 hour, but don't put them in the fridge or the caramel may soften if left too long.

note Traditional mini-cazuelas are made of terracotta, and are widely available in kitchen shops and Spanish delis.

coffee crèmes brûlées

500 ml single cream
5 teaspoons instant coffee granules
8 tablespoons caster sugar
4 egg yolks
2 tablespoons plain flour
1 tablespoon brandy

4 small ramekins
a cook's blowtorch (optional)

serves 4

A crisp, glossy, burnt sugar crust tops a creamy, coffee-flavoured custard. Sheer heaven and an impressive dinner party dessert.

Put the cream, coffee granules, and half the sugar in a saucepan and warm gently until the coffee and sugar have dissolved, then remove from the heat.

Put the egg yolks in a bowl and whisk in the flour until the mixture is smooth. Gradually whisk in the warm coffee cream mixture, then return to the saucepan. Heat very gently, stirring, for 5–10 minutes until you get a thick custard.

Stir in the brandy, then pour the custard into the ramekins. Let cool, then cover and chill for at least 2 hours or overnight.

When you are ready to serve the crèmes brûlées, preheat the grill to high. Sprinkle each one with 1 tablespoon of the remaining sugar and place under the grill for about 5 minutes, until the sugar melts and caramelizes.

Remove from the heat, chill for a minute or two to set the brûlée, then serve. (If you have a cook's blowtorch, use this instead of the grill to caramelize the sugar.)

honey & pistachio panna cotta

7 g powdered gelatine (1 sachet)
200 ml double cream
250 g Greek-style yoghurt
25 g caster sugar
6 tablespoons clear honey
50 g ground almonds
1 vanilla pod, split lengthways
watermelon slices, to serve (optional)

4 metal or china ramekins, lightly oiled and lined with muslin or clingfilm

serves 4

Here is a very pretty yet simple pudding you can make in advance of a party. If you don't have individual ramekins, you can use one large mould – a glass bowl will do.

Put 3 tablespoons warm water in a small bowl, sprinkle the gelatine evenly over the top and leave until dissolved, about 5 minutes.

Put the cream in a mixing bowl. Add the yoghurt, sugar and honey and stir until smooth. Mix in the ground almonds.

Scrape the vanilla seeds out of the pod, then stir them into the cream mixture. Add the gelatine.

Pour the cream mixture into the prepared ramekins, then chill for 4 hours or until set.

To serve, carefully turn out onto small serving plates. Accompany with slices of watermelon or other fresh fruit of your choice.

vanilla ricotta creams with saffron-poached pears

6 unripe pears, peeled
400 ml dry cider
4 tablespoons clear honey
½ vanilla pod
a pinch of saffron threads
1 unwaxed lemon
1 tablespoon arrowroot or cornflour

ricotta creams
300 ml skimmed milk
14 g powdered gelatine
(2 sachets)
60 g caster sugar
½ vanilla pod
250 g ricotta
100 g low-fat natural yoghurt

6 small pudding basins

serves 6

These little set ricotta creams are similar to traditional Italian panna cotta, but lighter and lower in fat. They make the perfect accompaniment for the tender pears in rich sauce.

Take a thin slice off the base of each peeled pear so that it can stand upright. Put the pears in a saucepan with the cider, honey, vanilla pod, saffron threads and 100 ml water. Pare 4 strips of zest from the lemon and squeeze out the juice. Add both to the pan. Cover and bring to the boil. Simmer gently, covered, for about 40 minutes or until the pears are tender and look slightly translucent. Turn the pears a couple of times during cooking so that they cook and colour evenly, as the poaching liquor won't cover them completely.

While the pears are cooking, make the ricotta creams. Measure 4 tablespoons of the milk into a small bowl and sprinkle over the gelatine. Set aside for 5 minutes to swell. Meanwhile, put the remaining milk in a saucepan with the sugar and vanilla pod. Slowly bring to a simmer, then remove from the heat. Stir the gelatine into the hot milk until dissolved. Let cool slightly.

Mix the ricotta and yoghurt together until smooth. Gradually blend in the milk, discarding the vanilla pod. Divide the mixture between the pudding basins and let cool, then cover and chill for 2–3 hours.

When the pears are tender, transfer to a dish. Blend the arrowroot or cornflour with a little cold water, then stir this into the poaching liquor. Heat, stirring constantly, until thickened, then pour over the pears and let cool. To serve, turn the ricotta creams out and place each one in a shallow bowl. Serve with a poached pear, in a pool of the golden sauce.

cranberry & raspberry jellies

10 g sheet gelatine
or 3 teaspoons powdered gelatine
500 ml cranberry juice
25 g caster sugar
8 cloves
1 cinnamon stick
6 slices fresh ginger
125 g fresh or frozen raspberries

4 glasses or glass serving bowls

serves 4

Jelly isn't just for kids! These ruby-coloured jellies make a light and refreshing treat and are a good choice for the more health-conscious dessert lover.

Put the gelatine sheets in a bowl of cold water to soften for 5 minutes. Put the cranberry juice, sugar and spices in a saucepan and bring to the boil. Simmer gently for 2–3 minutes, then remove from the heat. Squeeze the excess water from the gelatine, then add to the hot spiced cranberry juice, where it will melt almost instantly. Let cool.

Divide the raspberries between 4 glasses and strain the cooled jelly on top. Cover with clingfilm and chill for about 3 hours or until set.

If using powdered gelatine, measure 4 tablespoons of the cranberry juice into a small bowl and sprinkle the gelatine over the liquid. Leave to swell for 5 minutes while you simmer the remaining cranberry juice, then stir into the hot liquid until dissolved. Let cool and continue as above.

sparkling nectarine
& blueberry jellies

10 g sheet gelatine
or 3 teaspoons powdered gelatine
500 ml sparkling peach-flavoured wine
3 ripe nectarines
2 tablespoons freshly squeezed
lemon juice
200 g fresh blueberries, rinsed

*8 glasses or small glass
serving dishes*

serves 8

Wine and fresh fruit jellies are a sophisticated treat and look spectacular when made in glasses. They are the perfect choice for summer entertaining.

Put the gelatine in a flat dish and sprinkle over 4 tablespoons cold water. Leave to soak for 3 minutes until soft.

Heat the wine, either in a microwave or saucepan, until hot but not boiling. Tip the gelatine into the wine and stir to dissolve, then set aside to cool.

Cut the nectarines into cubes and sprinkle with the lemon juice. Put a few blueberries and cubes of nectarine in the bottom of each glass then pour over the jelly mixture to cover. Put in the fridge to chill.

As soon as the jelly has set, add the remaining fruit and jelly. Return to the fridge to set for another 45 minutes–1 hour before serving.

pink cava &
strawberry jellies

12 sheets of gelatine
(or enough to set 1.1 litres of liquid)
1.1 litres Cava Rosado
or other sparkling rosé
800 g fresh strawberries
2–3 tablespoons caster sugar, to taste
90–125 ml sugar syrup or gomme
pouring cream or vanilla ice cream,
to serve

*12 wine glasses or small glass
serving dishes*

serves 12

Everyone enjoys a glass of sparkling wine so these pretty jellies made with Spanish cava and fresh strawberries are guaranteed to be a hit.

Lay the gelatine sheets in a large shallow dish and sprinkle over 5–6 tablespoons cold water. Leave to soak for 3 minutes until soft. Heat the wine in a microwave or saucepan until hot but not boiling. Tip the soaked gelatine into the wine and stir to dissolve, then set aside to cool.

Hull and rinse the strawberries, cut them into halves or quarters to give even-sized pieces and put them into a shallow bowl, sprinkle over the sugar and leave them to macerate. Check the liquid jelly for sweetness, adding the sugar syrup to taste.

Divide half the strawberries between the serving glasses then pour over enough jelly to cover them. Put in the fridge to chill. As soon as the jelly has set (about an hour), add the rest of the fruit and jelly.

Return to the fridge to set for another 45 minutes–1 hour before serving with cream or ice cream.

frozen desserts

cherry fudge ice cream

250 g mascarpone cheese
250 ml full-fat milk
150 g caster sugar
200 g soft fudge,
cut into chunks
100 g glacé cherries, halved

an ice cream machine (optional)

serves 4–6

What makes this ice cream such a winner is the generous speckling of chewy fudge and cherries dotted throughout.

Put the mascarpone, milk and sugar in a bowl and whisk until smooth. Transfer the mixture to an ice cream machine and churn until almost frozen.

Add the fudge pieces and the chopped cherries and continue churning until the mixture is completely frozen. Transfer to a sealable freezerproof container and freeze until ready to serve.

You can also make the ice cream without a machine. Simply follow the instructions given below, folding in the fudge pieces and chopped cherries before returning the ice cream to the freezer for the final time.

The mixture should be frozen in a shallow container. When almost solid, beat it well with a wire whisk or electric beater until smooth, then return to the freezer. Repeat the process twice more, to break down the ice crystals, and the result will be a smooth ice cream.

Transfer the ice cream to the fridge for 20–30 minutes before serving, to let it soften evenly throughout. Homemade ice cream is best eaten as soon as possible after being made, and certainly within a week.

chocolate chip cookie ice cream

250 g mascarpone cheese
250 ml full-fat milk
100 g light muscovado sugar
150 g chocolate chip cookies,
crumbled

an ice cream machine (optional)

serves 4–6

Choose good-quality cookies, made with butter if possible – and of course, plenty of real chocolate chips. Cheaper cookies will spoil the ice cream by giving it a greasy aftertaste when frozen.

Put the mascarpone, milk and sugar in a bowl and whisk until smooth. Transfer the mixture to an ice cream machine and churn until almost frozen.

Fold in the crumbled cookies and continue churning until the mixture is completely frozen. Transfer to a sealable, freezerproof container and freeze until ready to serve.

You can also make the ice cream without a machine. Simply follow the instructions given below, folding in the crumbled cookies before returning the ice cream to the freezer for the final time.

The mixture should be frozen in a shallow container. When almost solid, beat it well with a wire whisk or electric beater until smooth, then return to the freezer. Repeat the process twice more, to break down the ice crystals, and the result will be a smooth ice cream.

Transfer the ice cream to the fridge for 20–30 minutes before serving, to let it soften evenly throughout. Homemade ice cream is best eaten as soon as possible after being made, and certainly within a week.

new york cheesecake ice cream

100 ml full-fat milk
100 ml double cream
4 egg yolks
150 g caster sugar
300 g cream cheese
grated zest and freshly squeezed juice of 2 unwaxed lemons
100 g oat cookies, crumbled into small pieces
Strawberry Sauce (page 233), to serve (optional)

an ice cream machine (optional)

serves 4–6

All the flavours of a luscious, lemony New York cheesecake, right down to the crunch of the cookie base. Don't be tempted to use low-fat cream cheese – the flavour and texture won't be the same.

Pour the milk and cream into a saucepan and heat to boiling point.

Put the egg yolks and sugar in a bowl and beat until pale and creamy. Pour the hot liquid over the eggs, stir until smooth, then pour back into the saucepan. Turn down the heat and cook over low heat, stirring constantly with a wooden spoon, until the custard has thickened enough to leave a finger trail on the back of the spoon. Take care that the mixture doesn't overheat and scramble.

Remove from the heat and let cool completely. Beat in the cream cheese and the lemon juice and zest until smooth. Churn in an ice cream machine until the mixture is almost frozen. Add the crumbled cookies and continue to churn until it is completely frozen. Transfer to a sealable freezerproof container and freeze until ready to serve.

You can also make the ice cream without a machine. Simply follow the instructions given below, folding in the crumbled cookies before returning the ice cream to the freezer for the final time.

The mixture should be frozen in a shallow container. When almost solid, beat it well with a wire whisk or electric beater until smooth, then return to the freezer. Repeat the process twice more, to break down the ice crystals, and the result will be a smooth ice cream.

Transfer the ice cream to the fridge for 20–30 minutes before serving, to let it soften evenly throughout. Homemade ice cream is best eaten as soon as possible after being made, and certainly within a week. Serve generous scoops, drizzled with Strawberry Sauce, if liked.

apricot ice cream

250 g mascarpone cheese
200 ml full-fat milk
100 g caster sugar
250 g apricot conserve

an ice cream machine (optional)

serves 4–6

This is such an easy recipe to make. The quality of the conserve is crucial to the recipe's success: always check the label, and choose a first-rate conserve with at least 55 g of fruit in every 100 g of jam.

Put the mascarpone, milk, sugar and 200 g of the conserve in a bowl and whisk until thick and smooth.

Churn in an ice cream machine until almost frozen, then fold in the remaining apricot conserve to give a ripple effect. Continue churning until completely frozen. Transfer to a sealable freezerproof container and freeze until ready to serve.

You can also make the ice cream without a machine. Simply follow the instructions given below, folding in all the remaining apricot conserve before returning the ice cream to the freezer for the final time.

The mixture should be frozen in a shallow container. When almost solid, beat it well with a wire whisk or electric beater until smooth, then return to the freezer. Repeat the process twice more, to break down the ice crystals, and the result will be a smooth ice cream.

Transfer the ice cream to the fridge for 20–30 minutes before serving, to let it soften evenly throughout. Homemade ice cream is best eaten as soon as possible after being made, and certainly within a week.

malted chocolate ice cream with rich chocolate fudge sauce

Rich Chocolate Fudge Sauce
(page 229)
300 ml double cream
300 ml full-fat milk
100 g instant malted drink powder
(such as Ovaltine, Horlicks
or Bournvita)
75 g dark chocolate (60–70% cocoa
solids), grated
6 egg yolks
175 g unrefined caster sugar
2–3 tablespoons chocolate liqueur
(optional)

an ice cream machine (optional)

serves 6–8

This is just about the richest, most luscious ice cream you will ever taste, conjuring up childhood memories of hot drinks by the open fire. Don't use your very best dark chocolate for this – it will be wasted.

Put the cream and milk in a pan and bring to the boil. Remove from the heat and whisk in the malted powder. Add the chocolate and stir until melted.

Using an electric whisk, whisk the egg yolks and sugar together until pale and fluffy. Pour in the malt mixture, stirring all the time until well blended. Return to the pan and cook for 5 minutes, or until slightly thickened – do not allow the mixture to get too hot or it will curdle. Remove the pan from the heat and leave to cool, stirring from time to time until cold. Add the liqueur, if using.

Churn the mixture in an ice cream machine in two batches. It will increase in volume as it thickens and freezes. Stop churning when thick and smooth, then transfer to a sealable freezerproof container and freeze. You can also make the ice cream without a machine. Simply follow the instructions given below.

The mixture should be frozen in a shallow container. When almost solid, beat it well with a wire whisk or electric beater until smooth, then return to the freezer. Repeat the process twice more, to break down the ice crystals, and the result will be a smooth ice cream.

Transfer the ice cream to the fridge for 20–30 minutes before serving, to let it soften evenly throughout. Homemade ice cream is best eaten as soon as possible after being made, and certainly within a week. Serve in scoops, drizzled with Rich Chocolate Fudge Sauce.

lemon curd ice cream

450 g homemade or good-quality bought lemon curd

250 ml whipping or double cream

3 tablespoons icing sugar, sifted

freshly squeezed lemon juice, to taste (optional)

an ice cream machine (optional)

serves 4–6

This really is a very simple ice cream and yet also very delicious. Use homemade curd or, at a pinch, the very best bought stuff. It goes very well with strawberries, tossed in a little sugar and a few drops of lemon juice.

Beat the curd smooth in a bowl, then lightly whip the cream until it just begins to thicken and leave a whisk trail. Sweeten the cream with the sugar, then gently fold the cream into the curd. Sharpen the taste with lemon juice, if you like.

Churn in an ice cream machine until completely frozen. Transfer to a sealable freezerproof container and freeze until ready to serve.

You can also make the ice cream without a machine. Simply follow the instructions given below.

The mixture should be frozen in a shallow container. When almost solid, beat it well with a wire whisk or electric beater until smooth, then return to the freezer. Repeat the process twice more, to break down the ice crystals, and the result will be a smooth ice cream.

Transfer the ice cream to the fridge for 20–30 minutes before serving, to let it soften evenly throughout. Homemade ice cream is best eaten as soon as possible after being made, and certainly within a week.

variation To make a Lemon Meringue Ice Cream remove the ice cream from the freezer halfway through the freezing process (allow 1½–2 hours) and stir the mixture. Stir in some crumbled bought meringue nests, leaving some of the meringue in quite large chunks. Continue to freeze, as above.

orange & mango freeze

4 large oranges, halved

2 large mangoes, peeled and stoned

2 tablespoons finely grated orange zest

3 tablespoons low-fat natural yoghurt

3 tablespoons low-fat crème fraîche

25 g dark chocolate, grated

serves 4

Here mango blends with yoghurt and crème fraîche to create a deliciously creamy dessert, just like ice cream but it's lower in fat and is a great way of upping your daily fruit intake!

Scoop out the flesh from the oranges, leaving the skins intact. If necessary, cut a small slice off the base of each orange half so that it stands upright.

Put the orange and mango flesh, orange zest, yoghurt and crème fraîche in a blender. Blend for a few minutes until smooth. Spoon the mixture into a freezerproof container and freeze for 2 hours, stirring occasionally to break up the ice crystals.

Spoon the mixture into the orange halves. Return to the freezer and leave for at least 1 hour, or until frozen solid. Let soften in the fridge for at least 30 minutes before serving. Serve 2 orange halves per person sprinkled with some freshly grated chocolate.

variation You could use pink grapefruit instead of the oranges; add 2 tablespoons of finely grated zest to the yoghurt mixture.

summer berry frozen yoghurt

500 g mixed summer berries, such as
strawberries, blackberries
and raspberries
150 g caster sugar
500 g full-fat plain yoghurt

an ice cream machine (optional)

serves 4

Use good, creamy, plain yoghurt for this recipe and you will be rewarded with a delectable dessert. A tart, low-fat yoghurt will give a sour, acidic flavour and an unpleasant, icy texture.

Warm the berries and sugar in a saucepan over low heat for several minutes, until the fruit begins to release its juices. Transfer to a food processor and blend to a purée. Push the purée through a fine-meshed nylon sieve to remove the seeds. Stir in the yoghurt.

Churn in an ice cream machine until almost frozen. Transfer to a freezerproof container and freeze until ready to serve.

You can also make the frozen yoghurt without a machine. Simply follow the instructions given below.

The mixture should be frozen in a shallow container. When almost solid, beat it well with a wire whisk or electric beater until smooth, then return to the freezer. Repeat the process twice more, to break down the ice crystals, and the result will be smooth and silky.

Transfer the frozen yoghurt to the fridge for 20–30 minutes before serving, to let it soften evenly throughout. Homemade frozen yoghurt is best eaten as soon as possible after being made, and certainly within a week.

honey parfait with meringue & caramelized pistachios

100 g shelled pistachio nuts
50 g caster sugar
300 ml whipping cream, chilled
2 large eggs, separated
100 g clear honey
6–8 meringue nests

a loaf tin or other freezerproof mould
6 glass serving dishes or glasses

serves 6

You don't need any special equipment to make a really fantastic frozen dessert, as this recipe will prove. It is also easy and quick to make. Freeze it in individual silicone moulds, if you prefer, but be sure to choose a shape that will allow for a meringue in the middle of each one.

Put the pistachios and sugar in a non-stick saucepan. Cook over medium-high heat, stirring, until they begin to caramelize. Remove from the pan and let cool. Grind coarsely in a food processor or by putting between 2 sheets of baking parchment and crushing with a rolling pin.

Put the cream in a large bowl and whisk until firm. Set aside. Put the egg yolks and honey in a second bowl, whisk well, then set aside. Put the egg whites in a third grease-free bowl and beat until they hold stiff peaks. Set aside.

Fold the egg yolk mixture into the cream until blended. Gently fold in the egg whites until just blended. Fold in the pistachios.

Spoon half the mixture into a freezerproof mould. Arrange the meringues on top in a single layer – nests may have to be broken up slightly depending on size, but not too small, because you want big pieces of meringue in the finished dish. Cover with the remaining parfait mixture and smooth the top. Cover with clingfilm and freeze until firm, about 6–8 hours or overnight. Scoop into tall glasses to serve.

chocolate liegeois

250 ml whipping cream, chilled
750 ml full-fat milk
4 scoops chocolate ice cream
4 scoops vanilla ice cream
flaked almonds, to serve

chocolate sauce
200 g sugar
80 g cocoa, plus extra for dusting
1 tablespoon instant coffee granules

4 tall glass serving dishes or glasses

serves 4

This French café classic is not quite a milkshake, not quite a sundae, and the result is something that is more grown-up than both. It is the ideal thing to serve for a large gathering or an al fresco meal. Do use good-quality ice cream.

To make the chocolate sauce, put the sugar and 350 ml water in a saucepan, stir, bring to the boil, then remove from the heat and stir in the cocoa and coffee. Let cool.

When ready to serve, whip the cream until firm.

Put the milk and the chocolate sauce in a jug or bowl and mix until well blended. Divide between 4 tall serving glasses.

Add 1 scoop each of chocolate and vanilla ice cream. Top each with a dollop of whipped cream and dust with cocoa. Sprinkle with the almonds. Serve with long spoons and straws.

coffee ricotta semifreddo

265 g chocolate digestives, chocolate chip cookies or bourbon biscuits

115 g unsalted butter

30 g soft brown sugar

350 g ricotta cheese, at room temperature

350 g mascarpone cheese, at room temperature

1 tablespoon dark rum

3 tablespoons Tía María or other coffee-flavoured liqueur

1 teaspoon vanilla extract

4 tablespoons icing sugar

125 g dark chocolate, grated

2 tablespoons ground Italian espresso coffee

shards made from 125 g chilled dark chocolate, to decorate

icing sugar, for dusting

whipped cream, to serve (optional)

*a springform cake tin,
25 cm diameter, lined*

serves 6–8

A semifreddo is a dessert that is half frozen to give it a slightly thickened, creamy texture. Ricotta and mascarpone are sweetened, laced with rum and Tía María, and flavoured with Italian coffee and grated plain chocolate. You must buy very finely ground espresso coffee, or it will taste gritty!

Put the biscuits in a food processor and blend until crumbs form. Alternatively, put the biscuits in a plastic bag and crush finely with a rolling pin. Melt the butter and sugar in a small saucepan over gentle heat. Stir in the crumbs and immediately press the crumb mixture into the base of the prepared cake tin. Chill until required.

Strain the ricotta cheese into a bowl, then beat in the mascarpone with a wooden spoon. Beat in the rum, liqueur, vanilla extract and sugar, then fold in the grated chocolate and coffee, leaving the mixture streaky. Carefully spoon into the prepared base.

Freeze for about 2 hours until just frozen. The dessert should be only just frozen or very chilled. Transfer to the fridge 30 minutes before serving to soften slightly if too firm.

To serve, unmould, remove the paper and set on a large serving plate. Use a knife to cut through very cold plain chocolate to make spiky shards, then use to cover the surface of the semifreddo. Dust with icing sugar and serve with a spoonful of whipped cream, if liked.

caramelized plum sorbet

1 kg red plums,
halved and stoned

2 tablespoons caster sugar

freshly squeezed juice
of ½ lemon

bought sweet almond wafer biscuits,
to serve (optional)

sugar syrup

300 ml caster sugar

1 vanilla pod, split lengthways

an ice cream machine (optional)

serves 6–8

A refreshing and summery sorbet – pretty and delicious when served with thin, crisp, almond biscuits. Roasting the plums before they are puréed will intensify their flavour.

Preheat the oven to 200°C (400°F) Gas 6.

Put the halved plums, cut-side up, in a baking dish, sprinkle with the sugar, and bake in the preheated oven for 20 minutes, until golden and softened. Let cool completely, then transfer to a blender and purée until very smooth. Stir in the lemon juice.

Meanwhile, to make the sugar syrup, put the sugar and vanilla pod into a saucepan, add 600 ml water, and heat gently until the sugar has dissolved. Bring to the boil, reduce the heat and simmer for about 5 minutes. Let cool, remove the vanilla pod, then stir the syrup into the plum purée.

Churn in an ice cream machine until frozen. Transfer to a sealable freezer-proof container and freeze until ready to serve.

You can also make the sorbet without a machine. Simply follow the instructions given below.

The mixture should be frozen in a shallow container. When almost solid, beat it well with a wire whisk or electric beater until smooth, then return to the freezer. Repeat the process twice more, to break down the ice crystals, and the result will be a smooth sorbet.

Transfer the sorbet to the fridge for 20 minutes before serving, to let it soften evenly throughout. Serve with almond biscuits, if liked.

piña colada sherbet

150 g unrefined caster sugar
1 ripe pineapple
200 ml coconut cream
6 tablespoons freshly squeezed
lime juice (2–3 limes)
4 tablespoons white rum
2 large egg whites, beaten
tropical fruit salad, to serve (optional)

an ice cream machine (optional)

serves 6–8

This is a cross between an ice cream and a sorbet. It makes a fantastically refreshing end to the meal. Don't make it more than a few days in advance though, as it won't keep well.

Put the sugar in a saucepan with 200 ml water and set it over very low heat. Stir occasionally, until the sugar has dissolved, then bring to the boil without stirring and boil for about 4 minutes. Let cool.

Quarter the pineapple, cut away the tough central core and cut off the skin. Cut into cubes and pass through a juicer.* This should give you about 550–600 ml juice. Mix in the coconut cream, cooled sugar syrup, lime juice and rum, which should give you just over 1 litre liquid.

Cover, transfer the sherbet mixture to the fridge and chill for a couple of hours. Pour into an ice cream machine and churn, adding the egg whites halfway through. If you haven't got an ice cream machine, pour the mixture into a sealable, freezer-proof container and freeze for about 1½ hours, or until beginning to harden at the edges. Put the egg whites in a food processor, process briefly until frothy, then tip in the half-frozen sherbet mixture and whizz until smooth. Return the sherbet mix to the freezer, freeze for another hour, then whizz again. Freeze and whizz a third time for extra smoothness. Leave to harden. Remove the sherbet from the freezer and transfer to the fridge for about 20 minutes before serving. Serve with a selection of tropical fruits.

* If you haven't got a juicer, remove all the little brown 'eyes' from the pineapple, cut into cubes, purée in a food processor or blender and strain the juice.

raspberry sherbet

120 g caster sugar
375 g raspberries
375 g fat-free fromage frais

an ice cream machine (optional)

serves 4–6

Pink, creamy and luscious – this sherbet sounds far naughtier than it actually is! Fresh berries and fat-free fromage frais make for a delightfully low-fat treat.

Gently heat the sugar and 100 ml water in a saucepan, stirring to dissolve the sugar. Bring to the boil and remove from the heat.

Purée the raspberries in a food processor or blender. Press through a nylon sieve to remove the seeds. Stir into the cold syrup and chill until very cold.

Add the fromage frais to the purée and whisk until smooth.

Churn in an ice cream machine until frozen. Transfer to a sealable freezer-proof container and freeze until ready to serve.

You can also make the sherbet without a machine. Simply follow the instructions given below.

The mixture should be frozen in a shallow container. When almost solid, beat it well with a wire whisk or electric beater until smooth, then return to the freezer. Repeat the process twice more, to break down the ice crystals, and the result will be a silky smooth.

Transfer the sherbet to the fridge for 20 minutes before serving, to let it soften evenly throughout.

lemon & raspberry iced vodka martinis

500 ml lemon sorbet
500 ml raspberry sorbet
1 bottle of frozen* vodka

4 Martini glasses,
frosted in the freezer
drinking straws

serves 4

Easy, light, stunning. Iced vodka Martinis are the perfect instant dessert, so long as you don't have too many of them!

Take the sorbets out of the freezer 20 minutes before you want to serve them and transfer to the fridge.

Scoop a couple of balls of sorbet into each glass (same flavour or mixed) and pour over a splash of ice-cold vodka. Serve immediately with small spoons and short drinking straws, if liked.

* Vodka won't actually freeze but keep it in the freezer and it will be wonderfully cold.

variation Try one of the many flavoured vodkas now available. Vanilla is delicious with strawberry or raspberry sorbet, or try citrus vodka with lemon or orange sorbet.

iced strawberry hearts

500 g fresh strawberries
75 g unrefined caster sugar
300 ml low-fat vanilla-
flavoured yoghurt

6 heart-shaped moulds

serves 6

The combination of strawberries and cream is a guaranteed favourite with everyone. Show them how much you care with this healthy version.

Wash, hull and roughly chop the strawberries. Place them with the sugar in a food processor or blender and whizz until smooth.

Fill the heart moulds to halfway up with strawberry purée and freeze for several hours or until set.

Top with the vanilla yoghurt and freeze until completely frozen.

Dip the moulds in hot water for a few seconds to unmould and serve immediately.

mixed berry iced soufflés

350 g mixed berries such as raspberries, strawberries and blackberries

120 g unrefined caster sugar

2 egg whites

55 g icing sugar

450 ml fromage frais

6 ramekins or short paper cups

serves 6

This is a dramatic and elegant frozen dessert which can be made well in advance so it's perfect for entertaining.

Make 6 strips of double-thickness greaseproof or parchment paper to form collars around the outsides of the ramekins, each coming 3 cm above the rim. Wrap and secure each collar with a pin or cocktail stick and chill the ramekins until ready to use.

Set aside 12 berries to decorate the soufflés. Purée the remaining berries in a food processor or blender and then press through a nylon sieve to remove the seeds. Stir in the caster sugar and set aside for at least 1 hour to allow the sugar to dissolve and the flavours to develop.

Whisk the egg whites until they form soft peaks, then add the icing sugar and continue to whisk until glossy and firm. Beat the fromage frais lightly just to loosen it.

With a large spoon or spatula gently fold the berry purée, egg whites and fromage frais together. Spoon into the prepared ramekins, smooth the tops and cover with foil, taking care that the foil does not touch the tops of the soufflés. Freeze until firm.

Remove from the freezer 5–10 minutes before serving and remove the foil and collars. Place in the fridge to soften for about 5 minutes and then decorate with the reserved berries to serve.

sauces, creams & custards

white chocolate sauce

This is one for all those who love white chocolate – it is very rich and sweet, so a little will go a long way.

250 ml single or double cream
100 ml milk
250 g white chocolate
(over 25% cocoa butter), chopped

makes about 600 ml

Put the cream and milk in a small saucepan and bring to just below boiling point. Remove from the heat and leave to cool for 2–3 minutes. Add the white chocolate and stir until completely melted. Serve warm.

If reheating, do so over gentle heat. Do not allow to boil or the sauce can thicken and seize.

bitter chocolate sauce

The flavour of this sauce will rely on the type of chocolate you use, so choose it carefully. You may like to add a little sugar to sweeten it.

225 g dark chocolate
(60–70% cocoa solids), grated
200 ml double or whipping cream
40 g unsalted butter, cubed

makes about 450 ml

Put the chocolate and cream in a small saucepan. Heat very gently, stirring occasionally, until melted and very smooth. Do not allow to boil. Whisk in the butter and serve warm.

rich chocolate fudge sauce

The only way to make a true fudge sauce is to include soft brown sugar. This gives it that fudgy taste and texture. It's best to use cocoa here, as the sauce is boiled and chocolate is too delicate to handle the heat.

175 ml double cream
150 g soft light brown sugar
50 g unrefined caster sugar
75 g cocoa, sifted
50 g unsalted butter, cubed
1 teaspoon vanilla extract
a pinch of salt

makes about 450 ml

Put the cream, brown sugar, caster sugar and cocoa in a saucepan. Gradually bring to the boil, stirring occasionally. Turn down the heat and simmer gently for 1 minute, stirring to help the sugars dissolve. Stir in the butter, vanilla extract and salt. Serve warm.

blueberry sauce

In this tempting sauce, fresh blueberries are simmered until they burst and release their juices and luscious flavours. Serve with cream-based puddings such as panna cotta or lemon mousse.

350 g fresh blueberries
3 tablespoons caster sugar
grated zest of ½ unwaxed lemon
a squeeze of fresh lemon juice

serves 4

Put the blueberries, sugar, lemon zest and 1 tablespoon water in a saucepan and heat gently until the sugar dissolves. Increase the heat slightly and simmer, partially covered, for 8–10 minutes, or until the berries soften and the sauce thickens up.

Remove from the heat and add the lemon juice. Serve hot or at room temperature.

melba sauce

Melba sauce is traditionally served with peaches and cream to make peach Melba, but it is equally delicious with any other fresh fruit, such as hulled strawberries. Serve with ice cream or fruit tarts.

250 g fresh raspberries
2 tablespoons kirsch
1–2 tablespoons icing sugar

serves 4–6

Put all the ingredients in a food processor or blender and whizz until smooth. Pass the purée through a nylon sieve and serve.

passion fruit sauce

This tangy passion fruit syrup is sublime poured over lemon mousse, vanilla ice cream or fresh fruit pavlova. The sweetest, ripest passion fruit have a very dimpled skin – be sure to buy them like this.

100 g caster sugar
75 ml passion fruit pulp
(from about 6 passion fruit)

serves 4

Put the sugar and 100 ml water in a saucepan and heat gently until the sugar dissolves. Add the passion fruit pulp, bring to the boil, then simmer gently for about 10 minutes, or until the fruit mixture is reduced slightly and has thickened. Leave to cool and serve at room temperature.

strawberry sauce

A delicious sauce that's perfect with cheesecake and ice cream.

500 g fresh strawberries
2 tablespoons icing sugar
1 tablespoon balsamic vinegar

makes about 300 ml

Hull and halve the strawberries, then put them in a small saucepan with the icing sugar and 3 tablespoons water. Heat slowly until the juices start to run, then transfer to a blender or food processor, add the balsamic vinegar and purée until smooth. If you prefer, press the sauce through a sieve to remove the seeds. Pour into a small bowl, cover with clingfilm and chill until required.

variation Make raspberry sauce the same way, but substitute raspberry vinegar for the balsamic vinegar – it just adds a certain sharp note to the sauce.

mascarpone cream

Creamy, indulgent, rich and heavenly with baked peaches.

500 ml mascarpone cheese
or double cream
3 tablespoons icing sugar
100 ml Italian Vin Santo
or Marsala wine

makes about 500 ml

Put the mascarpone cheese, icing sugar and Vin Santo in a large bowl and, using a balloon whisk or electric hand mixer, whisk until soft peaks are formed.

Chill until required.

lemon syllabub cream

Good enough to eat on it's own but try it with fresh berries.

finely grated zest and juice of
1 unwaxed lemon
6 tablespoons Madeira wine
or sherry
150 ml dry white wine
freshly grated nutmeg
500 ml double cream
icing sugar, to taste

makes about 500 ml

Put the lemon zest in a bowl with the Madeira, wine and nutmeg. Leave to macerate for at least 1 hour. Strain into another bowl.

Put the cream and icing sugar to taste in another bowl, and using a balloon whisk or electric hand mixer, whisk until just starting to thicken, then gradually whisk in the flavoured wine until the mixture forms soft peaks. Use immediately, otherwise it will separate.

chocolate custard

The classic sauce for steamed puddings is guaranteed to become a family favourite. Serve it with vanilla sponge.

450 ml full-fat milk
3 tablespoons cocoa powder
60 g caster sugar
1 tablespoon cornflour
2 egg yolks

serves 4–6

Put all but 2 tablespoons of the milk into a large, heavy-based saucepan and heat until almost boiling. Sift the cocoa, sugar and cornflour into a heatproof bowl, stir in the egg yolks and the 2 tablespoons cold milk to form a thick paste, then stir in the hot milk. Strain the mixture back into the saucepan and stir constantly over low heat until the mixture thickens – do not let the mixture boil or it will curdle.

Remove from the heat and use immediately, or keep it warm until ready to serve.

crème anglaise

Crème anglaise or real custard should be stirred constantly over very gentle heat otherwise the egg yolks can curdle.

600 ml full-fat milk
1 vanilla pod, split lengthways
6 egg yolks
2 tablespoons caster sugar

serves 8–10

Put the milk and vanilla pod in a saucepan and set over very gentle heat until it reaches boiling point. Remove from the heat and set aside to infuse for 20 minutes, then discard the vanilla pod.

Whisk the egg yolks and sugar together until pale and creamy, then stir in the infused milk. Return to the pan and cook, stirring constantly with a wooden spoon. Do not let the sauce boil.

When the mixture has thickened so that it coats the back of the spoon, remove from the heat. Serve hot or cold.

sabyon

Sabayon is commonly flavoured with kirsch, a cherry liqueur, but other liqueurs such as Grand Marnier or amaretto can be used. This heavenly mousse-like sauce is perfect for blanketing summer fruits.

4 egg yolks
50 g caster sugar
2 tablespoons kirsch
1 vanilla pod, split lengthways

serves 4

Put the egg yolks, sugar and kirsch in a glass bowl and scrape in the seeds from the vanilla pod. Set the bowl over a pan of gently simmering water (do not let the bowl touch the water). Using an electric whisk, whisk the mixture constantly for 5–6 minutes, or until it thickens and the whisk leaves a ribbon-like trail across the surface.

Serve warm.

index

recipe credits

Fiona Beckett

Blueberry cheesecake
Grape and mascarpone tart
Hazelnut, chocolate and cardamom cream pie
Lemon and raspberry iced vodka martinis
Orange and Cointreau syllabub
Passionfruit pavlovas
Piña colada sherbet
Pink cava and strawberry jellies
Raspberry, apple and almond crumble
Raspberry and brown sugar meringues
Strawberry, rose and rhubarb fool
Strawberry tiramisù
Sparkling nectarine and blueberry jellies

Susannah Blake

Cappuccino cheesecake
Coffee crème brulées
Mocha fudge cake
Praline profiteroles
Sticky toffee pudding

Tamsin Burnett-Hall

Cranberry and raspberry jellies
Orange and sultana pudding with cardamom
Rhubarb and apple crumble
Vanilla ricotta creams with poached pears

Maxine Clark

American pie crust
Apricot and almond slump
Blackcurrant lake cheesecake
Bitter chocolate sauce
Black forest soufflé
Blueberry and sour cream pie
Coffee ricotta semifreddo
Cranberry and orange streusel crisp
Chocolate and strawberry pavlova
French apple tart
Fresh raspberry tart
Honey hazelnut crunch cheesecake
Individual maple and pecan cobblers
Lemon syllabub cream
Malted chocolate ice cream
Mango mousse with tropical fruit salad
Mascarpone cream
Mint chocolate mousse
Mixed nut treacle tart
Nectarine and ginger crumble
Pâté brisée
Pumpkin pie
Rich shortcrust pastry
Rich chocolate fudge sauce
Ricotta and muscatel raisin cheesecake
Strawberry sauce
Summer berry cobbler
Tarte Tatin
Toffee banana crumbles
White chocolate sauce

Linda Collister

Apple strudel
Baked alaska
Black forest gâteau
Chocolate amaretto torta
Chocolate and berry roulade
Chocolate soufflé
Classic chocolate mousse
Chocolate custard sauce
Mississippi mud pie

Ross Dobson

Almond and blood orange syrup cake
Apple and blueberry tarts
Baked lemon pudding
Cherry and almond clafoutis
Chocolate orange mousse
Fig and honey croissant pudding
Fresh fig and walnut meringue
Peach and raspberry scone cake
Poached pear tiramisù
Strawberry buttermilk cake
Strawberry meringue roulade

Liz Franklin

Cherry fudge ice cream
Chocolate chip cookie ice cream
Easy apricot ice cream
New York cheesecake ice cream
Summer berry frozen yoghurt

Brian Glover

Classic tarte au citron
Key lime pie
Lemon curd ice cream
Lemon and ginger cheesecake
Lemon meringue pie
Sweet tart pastry

Clare Gordon-Smith

Hazelnut roulade
Rhubarb galette

Rachael Anne Hill

Orange and mango freeze
Summer pudding

Jennifer Joyce

Apple pie

Louise Pickford

Blueberry sauce
Bread and butter pudding
Caramelized plum sorbet
Crème Anglaise
Melba sauce
Meringues with rosewater cream
Passionfruit sauce
Sabayon

Linda Tubby

Crema Catalana

Fran Warde

Banoffi pie
Honey and almond panna cotta
Lemon polenta cake
Steamed syrup pudding
Tiramisù
Vin santo trifle
Warm chocolate pudding

Laura Washburn

Almond meringue and chocolate layer cake
Crème caramel
Chocolate liegeois
Floating islands
Honey parfait
Peach cobbler
Raspberry cream
Rice pudding
Vanilla orange soufflé

Lindy Wildsmith

Blueberry fool

Sunil Vijayaker

Iced strawberry hearts
Mixed berry iced soufflés
Raspberry sherbet

photography credits

Key: a=above, b=below, r=right, l=left, c=centre.

Martin Brigdale

Endpapers, pages 4-5, 6al, 6ac, 8-9 background, 8l, 9, 13, 14, 22, 34, 37, 38, 45, 46-47 background, 72, 79, 86-87 background, 86c, 96, 99, 103, 104, 107, 108, 112, 115, 116, 120-121 background, 130, 133, 142, 146, 148-149 background, 149, 150, 158, 161, 174, 177, 178, 190-191 background, 190r, 208, 211, 212, 220, 226-227 background

Peter Cassidy

Pages 3r, 6cl, 7b, 8r, 10, 21, 30, 46l, 46c, 46r, 48, 51, 52, 56, 60, 63, 64, 76, 125, 126, 129, 145, 148c, 153, 162, 165, 173, 186, 189, 200, 216, 226l, 228

Richard Jung

Pages 1, 3cr, 6ar, 17, 26, 33, 75, 80, 83, 88, 92, 95, 119, 120l, 120r, 121, 137, 138, 141, 148l, 148r, 154, 170, 190c, 191, 203, 219, 223, 224, 226r

Debi Treloar

Pages 6c, 6cr, 6bc, 6br, 7a, 18, 68, 71, 166, 169, 181

Ian Wallace

Pages 3cl, 6bl, 120c, 122, 215, 226c, 227, 231, 232, 235

William Lingwood

Pages 2, 190l, 192, 195, 196, 199, 207

David Munns

Pages 8c, 47, 59, 111

William Reavell

Pages 55, 67, 182, 185

Polly Wreford

Pages 3l, 86l, 86r, 134

Philip Webb

Pages 7c, 29, 100

Caroline Arber

Pages 87, 91

Nicki Dowey

Pages 84, 204

Noel Murphy

Pages 41, 157

Jean Cazals

Page 43

Vanessa Davies

Page 25